Special Gifts

*Women Writers on
the Heartache, the Happiness and the Hope
of Raising a Special Needs Child*

Thanks for all
you do for us
moms & kids! ☺

faith Gallatin
(B183)

Special Gifts

*Women Writers on
the Heartache, the Happiness and the Hope
of Raising a Special Needs Child*

ARLENE SCHUSTEFF

Wyatt-MacKenzie Publishing, Inc.
DEADWOOD, OREGON

Special Gifts: Women Writers on the Heartache, the Happiness and the Hope of Raising a Special Needs Child
by Arlene Schusteff

Wyatt-MacKenzie Publishing, Inc.,
Deadwood, Oregon
www.WyMacPublishing.com
(541) 964-3314

Requests for permission or further information should be addressed to:
Wyatt-MacKenzie Publishing, 15115 Highway 36,
Deadwood, Oregon 97430

Printed in the United States of America

Special Gifts
Table of Contents

Thump

Lisa Romeo

We sit in the family room, my son and I, discussing girls. He is twelve and I am taken aback, have to actually catch my breath and fight a suffocating pull, out of the room, into the past. What astonishes me is not that he is interested in girls, but that he is interested in girls at exactly the usual time in a young boy's life. He is not lagging behind by a year or more, or analyzing it dispassionately, in a manner beyond his chronological age, like when he was six and was passionate about fire trucks, not because they were shiny and red and loud, but because they had different pumping capacities. Now, he is telling me about how everyone in sixth grade loves Mr. Z, the new thirty-something music teacher. Mr. Z is "cool" and "seems like a kid too." It turns out Mr. Z is first and always, a drummer, and so for the first time at the middle school concert, beginning drummers, including Sean, will perform as a group. (When Mr. Z later tells me he was a first-class dyslexic ADD geek in middle school, I want to hug him.)

A week later, I am fidgeting and twisting in my seat, glancing to where the drummers and vocalists wait on the bleachers for the brass ensemble to finish up. I notice that, just like the other five drummers, Sean is talking and joke-punching, and twirling (and not dropping!) his drumsticks. He seems tall and so slender in his dress black pants and white button down shirt and tie; all legs and energy. If he is nervous and unsure, so are the others. He does not stand out. Before he plays even one beat, I am already happy for him in a way only my heart recognizes. It has been a long road and we are not anywhere near the end, but there were many days when I worried my different drummer would forever march on the sidelines.

This should be a happy time. Sean has outgrown, conquered and been "therapied out of" nearly all his issues. At least that is how it appears. So I must let him be. But even nearly normal can be scary, too. As the mother of a child who needs you more than normal, there comes a time, if we are lucky and blessed and have done our jobs, when his neediest needs have been met, when his being different subsides. Then what?

They are all ready to let him go. The psychologist, the learning consultant, the child study team, all the therapists. They tell me I should do likewise. Even the pediatric neurologist is done with him; the same doctor who told me that although Sean's particular brand of neurological impairment was probably lifelong, in time, maybe by adolescence, he would be "intact," would have learned to cope (or more likely, to mask) any lingering quirks and odd behaviors. I should not be surprised by this turn of events; that Sean has done just what the neurologist predicted, but I am.

For me, all the years of his being *not ready* still exist; clear and big, stacked in my mind (my heart) like so many hefty volumes, accumulating dust but still there, available, and full of so much hurt. Perhaps in Sean's mind it was nature or biology or God or luck that pushed those memories to a far-off corner, to be visited maybe only years from now, when normal is nothing new. Sean is as ready to test himself alone, as any other twelve year-old.

I began to wonder about my son's development by six months when he could not roll over; and at 18 months when he was uninterested in climbing out of the crib; and at two-and-a-half, when I kept waiting for him to "get into everything" and have tantrums. Sean got into exactly nothing. Asked to stay on the couch with a pile of picture books, that is just what he did. In a house with a toddler, we did not need cabinet locks, never hid the Pine-Sol. He never ventured, did not touch anything not presented as a toy, flushed nothing down the toilet. I kept waiting for him to unload his drawers in a heap or yank down the curtains or drop the remote control in the fish tank. A nervous new mother, naïve and hopeful, I listened to the pediatrician who assured me that Sean was developing at his own pace and that I was reading too many books. I knew something was amiss, but I was paralyzed. I wanted to know, and, I wanted to know nothing.

Finally, Sean's pre-school teacher took me aside: "I think Sean has developmental issues; you should have him evaluated." She had a list of examples, not that I needed any. *He knocks down playmates' block towers because he wants to play and cannot work out how to join the activity. He stands too close in line, yet is fearful of bumping another child. He cannot hold a scissor, appears ambidextrous but is uninterested in crayons, lines up toys in rows instead of playing with them.*

Soon after, I listened to a pediatric neurologist tick off a list that included fine and gross motor skill delays, visual and oral motor skill delays, speech abnormalities, auditory processing and motor planning delays, listening comprehension and Sensory Integration Dysfunction.

"He does all that hand-flapping and lining things up. Is he autistic?" I asked. *Well, no.* "He's so verbal and analytical and can't figure out gestures or other kids' body language. Could he have Asperger's Syndrome?" *Sort of, but no.* "Does he have Pervasive Developmental Delay?" *Close, but not precisely.* My son fell into the abyss between diagnoses. "Let's not worry about a diagnosis, just get him what he needs," Dr. Patel advised. What he needed was therapy, all kinds.

Sean defied categorization. Relatives and friends, especially other moms, saw the upside: He would not be labeled. But I wanted answers, concrete ones, a roadmap and a glance into the future. I called my cousin Lisa, whose son Luke, two years older than Sean, had strikingly similar symptoms. She told me she was sending something and the next day, the FedEx guy handed me a thin package, but instead of a book or list of specialists, only a single sheet of stiff cream parchment slid out, with that familiar — and nauseatingly cloying and trite poem — about marching to the beat of a different drummer. I thought it was drivel and put it in a cheap gold frame.

I read, hungrily and constantly about autism, Asperger's Syndrome, and PDD, devouring academic texts, practical guides, everything. I reasoned that if he shared so many behaviors with children firmly diagnosed as Asperger's or as extremely high functioning autistic, why not try what worked for them? It was in the anecdotal wisdom of other mothers of autistics, that I found how to fill in the spaces therapy could not. Writer-Mothers like Catherine Maurice (*Let Me Hear Your Voice*), and Beth Kephart (*A Slant of Sun*), who had improvised their own interventions were my guiding lights. One year, we tackled echolalia, when a child repeats back nearly verbatim, what you have just said.

"What do you want for breakfast?" I ask Sean.
"What do you want for breakfast?" Sean parrots.

"*I am asking what Sean wants to eat for breakfast.*"

"What Sean wants to eat for breakfast."

"*Don't repeat me.*" I say.

"Repeat me," Sean smiles.

"*Do you want oatmeal or waffles? Don't say anything else. Just say oatmeal or say waffles.*"

"Say oatmeal or say waffles."

"*Which do you want to eat – oatmeal or waffles?*".

"Eat oatmeal or waffles?"

"*Do you want oatmeal or waffles?*

"Oatmeal. Or. Waffles."

"*Waffles or oatmeal?*" I ask.

"Sean wants oatmeal," he says.

"*OK, we'll make oatmeal for breakfast.*"

"Oatmeal for breakfast."

"*Stop repeating.*"

"OK."

When we weren't doing at-home exercises, out we went to therapy four days a week in the morning and afternoon. Physical therapy. Occupational therapy. Visual therapy. Listening therapy. Speech. Social skills. We did speech therapy homework in the car. Sean would talk, I would listen. He would talk, I would correct. He would try again. The words, the sounds, were easy to hear. But I was listening for his heart. I wanted to know if it was breaking along with mine, but he remained cheerful, curious about therapy and interested in his therapists.

"We're going to therapy, right Mom?" Sean is eight.

"Right. Physical therapy today, with Alison. You get to ride the two-wheeler."

"Yeah, physical therapy today. I get to ride the bike. Alison is funny. She makes me laugh."

"Do you remember she said to look straight ahead all the time?"
"Yup, 'bike follows eyes.' Can we get a doughnut after?"

At five, Sean collected acorns alone at kindergarten recess, recoiling when kids scattered the nearby mulch during a game of tag that he did not know he should want to join. At seven (and eight and nine and ten) video games held no allure; and he was teased. We had to teach him things other kids pick up automatically, that some kids are bullies, that kids can pretend to be your friend then mock you, that you don't ask permission to play, you just do. He was a mini-adult in many ways, the playground police and kindness cop. When a boy once called Sean a "silly dumb doo-bop," I suggested he respond, "You're a silly dumb doo-bop, too." No, he said, "that might hurt his feelings." To the therapists, of course, this ability to anticipate another's emotional pain proved he could not be anywhere on the autism spectrum. I accepted that. I had plenty of other stuff to worry about.

By nine, my son's deficiency in reading social cues and interpreting body language led him into uncomfortable situations where he could not tell if he was wanted or hated. For a talkative little boy, there was an awful lot of silence. The party invitations not received, an empty playground corner that was full seconds before he arrived, the "hi's" and "hellos" that were missing when he joined the morning line.

We figured out how to help him stop the distracting hand flapping and the annoying spinning in place and the incessant talking that left teachers exasperated and prospective playmates bored. But it was another matter to teach a young boy how to be a kid. A little boy hungry for playmates, he was dependent on an alert teacher or aide.

"Connor, can you show Sean how to play that game?"

"Andrew, Sean wants to play too. Let's show him how , OK?"

Therapy, the at-home exercises, everything I read, it all worked. One by one, his "delays" got caught up and little by little, his differences became less apparent. We still ran interference for Sean, my husband and I (and teachers, counselors, coaches, *everyone*) dozens of times, anticipating awkward situations and trying, often awkwardly ourselves, to smooth the way. Many, many times it worked.

Occasionally it backfired and our hearts would break for him. His never did, however; he shrugged off slights and meanness and his classmate's crass disregard for his feelings. "They have the problem, not me," he would assert.

Through it all, Sean talked, to everyone who would listen. Even I got tired of hearing that lovely voice, my child's heart made verbal. Even now, on the cusp of being a teenager, Sean still loves talking, especially with adults. After one three-hour car trip, Sean talked so much I finally turned on him and snapped, "Sean, it's time to just shut up!"

At eleven, Sean started middle school a changed child. I worried that his heart made him too vulnerable, always wanting to help his classmates, not knowing what it meant to be used. Yet he figured it out, took some hits, rebounded; learned when to approach the school counselor, when to wait. I worried about logistics – Sean using a locker, navigating the larger building, late bells, walking two blocks to our spot in the car pick-up line. All this he managed and even made two new friends.

I think Sean decided on drum lessons partly as a release for the pre-adolescent tension of still being that slightest bit different, different in a way that only other pre-teens notice and persecute one another for. He said he just liked the sound, and that was good enough. Tone deaf and rhythmically challenged as I am, I stood by when he practiced at home, not realizing, as my musically-inclined husband did, that Sean often was off the count, ricocheting between too fast and too slow. I only knew that he was loving it. By December, he had gotten considerably better, my husband assured me. Good thing. I heard a concert was coming up.

I began to worry, as I always do, when Sean will be exposed to many people who do not know him or his story. How does a mother keep from believing that we should just continue to keep moving the net? Or are we done with all that because he no longer needs therapy, social skills training, listening exercises? Because he no longer spins in circles, arranges his toys in straight lines? Because he can cross the midline, keep his eyes focused on a tennis ball in play, walk into a new classroom without visiting it three times in advance, and tolerate a fire drill without screaming? If he is not transmitting the "I'm different" beacon anymore, is it really just a whole lot of coping? All the leftover vestiges of all the years of being different, to my eye and my sensibility, are all still plain. All the not fitting in, all the needing more and sometimes less, it is all still there, for me. That is a mom's territory, I suppose; knowing the crevices and dark corners where her child's molted skins lie.

Anyway what do I know? I know, for example, that his polite refusal of a cousin's hand-me-down Nintendo system is not what it seems; that once, exposure to the rapidly changing pixels of computer and video screens caused Sean's eyes true physical pain. It took three years, 158 sessions of ocular motor skill therapy, therapeutic eye-glasses, and vision exercises, for him to tolerate computer and TV screens, and not run screaming from the room if the picture sudden-ly rolled or jumped or a DVD sputtered or a website flashed away. Xboxes, Nintendo and the like, for the years when a boy might naturally gravitate to them, were agony.

Classmates still tease him for not being plugged-in. Once I suggest-ed he tell them it is because of weak eye muscles. "Are you kidding Mom? And give them something to be mean to me about?" Better they just think he is a little weird than that there is something quan-tifiably "wrong" with him. In middle school, he explains, being odd, weird or strange merely gets you teased; having "something wrong" means being ostracized, ignored or treated just a little too kindly.

Sometimes Sean wants to know what makes him different, why he needed so much therapy and special help. Occasionally he will ask a very specific question and I give him far too much information.

"Why can't I wear sun block that's tinted blue?" he asked once. *Because your skin is highly sensitive,* I tell him, *and that's why all the tags on your clothes bother you and you insist on tucking your PJs into your socks, and why it took us three years to get you to wash your hair under the shower head, and why you get upset every spring when it's time to stop wearing long sleeves, and why you hate to swap pants for shorts.*

"Why do loud noises bother me so much?" Sean wanted to know recently. *Your hearing is ultra-sensitive,* I said, *and that is why you cannot tolerate fireworks, and why you were the only child in elemen-tary school to get advanced warnings of fire drills, and why it took four tries and Grandpa's lawn-mowing ear protectors for you to go to the fireworks at the field behind our house instead of leaning awkwardly to catch a tree-studded glimpse from your bedroom window.*

Sean may not be so different now, but I can never be the mother of a child who did not struggle mightily, can never be the kind of mother without painful memories about ordinary moments. When Sean was two, he loved his Cozy Coupe, that quintessential little yellow and red plastic "car" in which toddlers tootle across driveways. But he did not scoot at all, never once, in fact, moved his little light-up Sesame Street sneakers. To him, the car was a bench. His occupational therapist taught him to move one foot at a time. I could see the wheels turning, not on the driveway, but in his small head – this foot, then that foot, then the first foot again, then the other. I turned away, exhausted.

These kind of memories, for me, exist together with the rest, the happy memories of his childhood, but I want them to disappear. I want to go back and to experience my own small child as others did, precocious, articulate, and bright, with cute little quirks. A good little boy who sometimes did odd things, but never misbehaved. I want to see him as full, complete, intact. Even today, I want him to be for me what he is to others, just a cheerful, dimpled pre-teen with a broad smile and bright eyes; the boy with the amazing vocabulary who can converse with adults astonishingly well.

Maybe I can't vanquish those memories because I could not confront it all as it was happening. Recently have I begun to answer truthfully, when asked why I closed my business and only take on only limited freelance work. "Because my child had neurological impairment and he needed me," I say now, instead of muttering that I wanted to spend more time with my children while they are young, which was also true, but incomplete.

This new "not-different" status maybe means that I too, can move on, or at least slightly away from, the role of mother-advocate, to simply, mother. It is a role not easy to relinquish. I was good, very good, at it. I got him through. The future? It is unknowable, even as we walk directly into its path. For right now, there is a middle school concert, a drum ensemble performance, another mile marker to approach, pass in a breath-holding instant, and bid farewell. I know that my son will move on, move ahead, with only the safety net that love and an understanding of the past (his and mine) can provide, and it just may be enough.

At the concert, the drummers play two songs, Sean making a few mistakes, but only about the same as the other novice drummers. It is time for the third song and they all have a smirk on. It is a simple rendition of "The Little Drummer Boy," thumped out with padded sticks on round tympani drums. *Pa Rum Pum Pum Pum.* Sean does not miss a single note; he is on time exactly each time, not fast, not slow. The song ends and the six drummers are still. Then they exchange a look with Mr. Z and as a group, with huge smiles, they all jump up straight and high on twelve gangly legs, and each brings down the padded stick in one resounding, purposeful boom. They have done it precisely, exactly, in unison; in sync. *Thump.* I smile at Sean and he smiles back, only not just at me, but I think maybe also at the girl in the next row, the one he used to push off the jungle gym in kindergarten.

The Juggler

Jesse Michener

She is fearless. A warrior-child whose battle is known to everyone but her. In her half-quiet world, she plugs along, making her own sense to things and ordering life perfectly. I marvel at her confidence and unabashed joy. I used to describe her personality as pure joy encased within one tiny body. She's older now and more reserved, but her confidence remains and glimpses of her joy still emerge frequently.

At the New Year's festival, she wants to volunteer in the juggling act. I know this because she raises her hand along with all of the other kids. At first I think she might be mimicking them, but after she persists, I know she understands. She wants to go on stage.

I cringe at the thought of the performer asking her her name. I imagine her silently smiling as he prods, "Little girl, what is your *NAME*?" "She's not stupid, you know," I'd yell. "She's half-deaf!" Worse, she might cry and not be able to see me over the stage lights. I'd be hidden among the hundreds of people and,oh god,she'd panic. How would I reach her with my two year-old hell-bent on proving her independence by running away from me at every turn and my nursling constantly attached to my breast?

She is resolute. She wants to be on the stage. I quickly coach her. "Violet, when he asks your name, you say, 'My-name-is-Violet.'"

"My name Bi-way," she responds.

"Yes, good. How old are you? Say 'I-am-four.'"

"I four. Mama ca I Bi-way tur?" She raises her hand in the middle of the act. Her eagerness once again comes at the wrong time. "Hold on, baby. Almost."

Too quickly, the juggling man thanks his volunteers on stage and announces he will need one more volunteer. Dutifully, I nudge Violet's hand in the air. She takes the cue with gusto. Hand up and chin forward, without being called on, she walks toward the stage, hand raised proudly in the air. She is out of my grasp and couldn't hear me if I called. Panic sets in. I can't save her anymore.

The world stops around me as my heart walks though the great crowd and up the stage steps. The performer laughs at her determination. "Well, okay, I guess we can have *two* volunteers." The crowd loves it. *Don't make her talk. Please,* I pray. Don't make her the fodder for the laughter of the unknowing.

"And what's your name?" he asks, shoving the microphone toward her mouth. I see her assess the situation and choose her response. "Aiee" She says with a grin.

"Ai—what?" He shakes his head. The crowd laughs, not knowing what to think.

"Ai—mee—cha" She says, smiling.

"How old are you, curly?" He asks, puzzled, ruffling her curly hair.

There is silence. Then, "Boo-laa laa."

The crowd quiets, just a little. They know. They get it but don't know what to think. The child is off. Something is off. They laugh. Of course they laugh.

I wonder if they know the terror I feel as she volunteers herself to be judged by the world. She knows nothing of evil. Knows nothing of suffering. She remains the center of her world, a world where she is the star of her show. I can only pray that when she awakens to *our* world, it is a gentle awakening. I pray she retains the confidence she has now as she stands up in front of the world, terrifyingly unapologetic.

"Ohhh-kay. I don't know what you're saying, but I like you!" the juggler says. He places her center stage with another, adult, a volunteer. I can tell he is worried she will screw up his act by not following directions. He has no idea if she understands what he is saying. She's a risk, for sure. She just smiles and makes faces at him. He, in turn, uses her oblivion as the punch-line to his antics. The audience just keeps on laughing.

"Stay there." He tells her. She responds by sticking out her tongue. He makes determined eye contact with his partner, offers a quick nod and they begin to juggle 12 pins around the two volunteers. She stands in the center, unfazed and unimpressed by the danger.

Her joy is remains pure and is contagious. Somehow, within that moment, I know with certainty that my girl will be okay. Not just for now, but for a lifetime. Standing in the center of life's great juggling act, daggers on all sides, *she'll* be the joy others seek out. Perhaps, if we are lucky, she'll share that world of hers with the rest of us. We need it.

Daniel's Gift

Kristen Scott

I thought I knew the answer to this one: *"If you could give any gift to anyone, what would it be?"*

I've often wished that I could give my son a normal life. I've wished that he could experience the fullness of the world the rest of us take for granted; normal communication and relationships, pursuing a career, falling in love, independence, learning to read.

If I could erase the effects of autism, make him a "normal" boy of almost 14, I'd do it in a heartbeat. Wouldn't I?

If I did it, he would be free then to engage fully in our world, to make decisions and follow his own path, solve his own problems and relish his victories. Free, as Thoreau implores us, to go confidently in the direction of his dreams, and live the life he imagines.

What would he be like, I wonder? I imagine him as a regular kid, hanging out at the mall with friends or playing Nintendo. I imagine him complaining about teachers and the indignity of homework, suffering through math tests and piano lessons and discovering girls.

I wonder if he would be an optimist, like his father, or more cautious, like me? An athlete or a scholar, or an artist like his grandparents?

Would we be saving for medical school or praying he graduates high school? Would he squabble with his sister and fight for the remote?

My son's concerns are much simpler, though: Will he be able to blow bubbles when he comes home from school, and watch his favorite videos? Will he get "fries, chicken and pop" when we go to Denny's, his favorite restaurant? Will I remember to close the garage door before we reach the end of the driveway?

He wants to be tickled and laughs joyfully. He loves school and buying his lunch in the cafeteria. After dinner he prompts me to wrap all leftovers and place them carefully in the refrigerator, whether they need refrigerating or not. Every night, he confirms that he'll go to school the next morning, with one of his few discernable words. "Bus?" he asks, secure in the answer, secure that his ordered world will not come to harm. His routines comfort him, providing a safe outline for his days. He goes to sleep each night untroubled by the concerns of our fuller lives, the entanglements of love and heartbreak and jealousy, of worry, resentment and loss. He is the happiest person I know.

Would I change him, if I could? Would I give him the "gift" of a normal life, and lose the person he is? This extraordinary child, whose idiosyncrasies and peculiarities are so dear to us, woven so intricately into the fabric of our family that we can't imagine it otherwise? Would I erase the impact of his disability on his older sister, a young woman of empathy and compassion, whose own life has been enriched beyond measure by her love for this unusual boy?

I'm glad these questions are merely fantasy, because I don't have an answer after all.

Children of the Night

Margaret Mitchell

Electronic hasps divide day from night. Impossibly pink and patron-izing. The receptionist assures me that nothing is out of the ordinary.

She doesn't have the black eye and the welt.

I sit in the mock living room till I can go back. The pallid man with a widow's peak and prominent cuspids tells me he has again lost his job and his apartment and asks how I'm doing. Dear God, tell me that wasn't some kind of pick-up line.

"No ring, I see." (Eew, it was.)
"What monster gave you that shiner?"
"My little boy, not even chest high."

Osteoporosis in a lab coat escorts me in past the rooms of people intoning the twelve steps like somber monks chanting. Past the mis-named "quiet room" with the urine-stained corner and the Plexiglas porthole.

This is where the werewolves are kept.

My child has been in here. Did he also mark it as his territory? And with a clatter of crayons there he is.

Mama! I want to come home, Mama.

I know, baby.

I want to come home!

I know, baby.

Please, Mama. I'll be good. I'm ready to come home.

Lip service to the mental health gods. The glint in his eye tells me the moon is waxing gibbous. The wrinkle between my eyebrows asks for the floor.

What will you do when he is six foot two?

Motion is seconded and ratified by the dark circles under my eyes.

I want you home when the doctor says…

Groundswell of rage. Mouth frothing. You wish I was dead! Ah, the silver bullet.

Visiting hours are over and I pry little fingers from my bruised and bitten wrist.

The heave and sweep of sobs or screams escape from me soundless on leather wings as sigh after sigh after sigh.

Before the Diagnosis

Michelle O'Neil

Every muscle in my body pulses with adrenaline as I dial the phone.

Rrrring..... Two rings. Three.

My hand shakes as I hold the receiver and say, "May I speak to Todd, please?" I smile through clenched teeth in hopes of sounding normal.

"I'm sorry sweetie, I can't hear you." says the motherly technician on the other end. "Is everything okay?"

She can't hear me because my two year-old daughter is shrieking.

"TODD, PLEASE." I yell into the receiver.

"Just a second," she replies coolly.

"Hello?" he says.

At the sound of his voice, I crumble to the floor. I try to speak but am reduced to jagged sobs.

"Sweetie, what is it? What happened?"

Suddenly I gulp air, stop crying, and hiss into the phone. "If you don't take me seriously, if we don't get some help, I swear you are going to come home to find her dead one day."

Silence.

I know it isn't fair to him. He's Chief Pharmacist at the hospital. He's got tons of responsibilities. He's working hard to support us. He's checking medications for an entire hospital population for God's sake. He needs to be focused. Sitting on the kitchen floor, I hold the phone to my ear with one hand and rest the other hand on my very pregnant belly.

"What happened?" he asks, softly.
I pause.

He isn't mad at me. Thank God he isn't mad at me.

I start, "Donna called and asked if we wanted to go to her pool. I packed everything up. I thought Riley would have fun. In the locker room Riley covered her ears and kicked and screamed as I tried to put on her bathing suit. She shrieked as we walked out toward the pool, screaming 'Too bright! Too bright!' When we got to the baby pool she didn't want to go in. She repeatedly tried to run away. I chased after her and carried her into the pool, sitting her on my lap. I thought she would get used to it. She proceeded to hit me in the face and scream. All the while, Donna just chattered away over her screams, oblivious. I swear, something about that woman makes her worse?"

I take another breath, then continue.

"There were tons of kids. All of them laughing and splashing. They were having a blast. How come anything that is supposed to be fun is miserable for her?"

"I don't know, doll." Todd says.

"After about five minutes of this I gave up. I took her out of the pool and sat her on a beach chair. As I was trying to gather our stuff, she swiped everything off the chair and into the pool. Our towels were soaked. I dragged her back into the locker room and she started screaming again. Everyone stared at us. They looked at me like I was a bad mother. Like she was a little brat."

"I'm so sorry honey." Todd says.

"When we got out to the car it was hot. She didn't want to get into her car seat. She screamed and flailed and as I tried to buckle her in, she kicked me in the face." I stop talking and close my eyes.
"Then what happened?"

"Honey…" my voice cracks. "I totally lost it on her."

"What did you do?" he asks softly.

Sobbing I tell him, "I got in her face. I screamed "SHUT UP! SHUT UP! And I smacked at her legs over and over. She looked up at me with pleading eyes. She cried and cried. People in the parking lot looked at me like I was a monster. I'm surprised they didn't call the cops." I wipe my nose with the back of my hand.

"I can't believe that was me. I told her to shut up? And I hit her? I can't believe I could get that angry. What's wrong with her? What's wrong with me? This isn't me, I'm telling you, something is terribly wrong. We need help."

Todd says, "I'll be home soon. I don't know what's wrong, but we're gonna figure this out."

I look at the clock. One more hour til' he gets off. We hang up. Riley has stopped shrieking and is playing happily with her toys on the floor in the next room. I'm astounded by the rage I feel toward her. She's over it, but I'm left with a splitting head and an aching body. My precious little girl. The child we wanted so much. This isn't what I signed up for at all.

Tunnel Vision

Julie Adams

Heartbreaking is the one word that pretty much sums up life with my son. Don't get me wrong, Michael is an awesome kid, and we love him greatly. He doesn't intend to break my heart, but watching him struggle and stumble through life, he does. I don't think there has been one single day in his entire life that I have not worried about him. He has officially been diagnosed with ADHD and OCD, and recently confirmed as having Asperger's syndrome and Bipolar tendencies. He is faced with more challenges than anyone should have to deal with. I pray every day that God will take away his difficulties.

I have found myself thinking that life would actually be easier on my child if he was born with a physical rather than a mental disability. Physical disabilities are visible, there are no questions. Physical disabilities are understood and forgiven. Since mental disabilities or personality disorders are largely misunderstood, they are rarely forgiven. Mental disabilities constitute behaviors that other children pick up on and make fun of. Personality disorders set a child apart. My son had friends in school until fifth grade when his fellow students stopped being understanding and no longer wanted anything to do with him. He became a social pariah, an outcast and a target for constant teasing and bullying. Sure, there were those that tolerated him during the day, maybe they were even nice to him. But, outside of school, no one wanted anything to do with him. Playdates were rare. The kids in the neighborhood stopped coming around. Since then, my heart has been breaking a little bit each day.

It's not easy to describe the pain I have experienced watching my son struggle through school. It is not easy to listen to what he encounters during the course of each day. Honestly, the misbehavior and the ADHD are a breeze to deal with compared to the social isolation. Now I know that social skills are just as important as intelligence, if not more so. You can teach someone to ride a bike, but you can't teach them how to react to falling off the bike or better yet, how to not react when someone laughs at them for falling. Social skills are impossible to teach. Trust me, we've tried.

We have spent more hours and money, too much to actually add up, trying to "fix" the behaviors that set him apart. Sure, his medication helps, but I've realized that no medication in the world can help when it comes social skills. I have found myself wondering lately if counseling has helped at all. He even said the other day that all the counselors tell him the same things just in different words. If all of his counselors have told him the same basic thing for the last six years and he's hasn't experienced improvement, what in the world have I been spending my money on?! We believe, or are lead to believe, that all professionals can help, but again I return to the same frustration that I started with, but with less money in my pockets.

Everyone wants their child to be accepted, to be welcomed into friendships, to get along with other kids. When it became obvious that this wasn't happening for Michael, we began our long road of interventions.

It's the same every year. School starts and we get through a couple of weeks and the pattern begins again. My heart aches and slowly breaks for my golden-hearted son who doesn't understand why his classmates mistreat him the way they do. He has had to learn way too early just how cruel people can be.

I can only hope that as he grows older, his peers will mature. Mature to an age when differences are embraced, not exploited and it is no longer sport to pick on others. I also hope that Michael will mature. I have to believe that one day all the prodding, pushing, guiding, talking, and praying will pay off. I just wish I knew when that light at the end of the tunnel would start to come into focus.

Loving Elena

Kimberly Winters

My husband and I share a running joke. "Please come back," he says each time I leave the house to return library books, buy bread for lunches the next day, or do some other errand that in all likeliness really doesn't need to be done that night.

Phil grins when he makes his plea, but this wasn't always the case. Used to be his eyes didn't match his smile. They'd cloud over and darken, almost as if he was worried I wouldn't return home.

Between you and me, his concern was well placed. Back then, I'd planned my escape more than once. "Don't worry," I say, fishing for my keys and hiking my purse over my shoulder. "I'll be back."

I've never given in to the urge to take a real walkabout—the kind that makes the network news at 6:00 and 10:00 p.m.— but I've come close. One dark day three winters ago stands out most vividly in my mind.

Ever since a ruptured brain aneurysm left my middle daughter Elena permanently disabled, a common cold can set her back two weeks or more. On the dark day in question, Elena was well into her second week of illness. Coughs racked her small body. Her fever neared 102 on Motrin. Antibiotics hadn't yet kicked in.

After holding one too many barf buckets, I collapsed on the sofa. Snow fell outside the front picture window, smothering the yard. I ached for the life we'd once had.

Elena was only nine when the aneurysm struck her down. Her older sister Liz was thirteen, her younger sister Sammi, five. We'd taken so much for granted back then; our home, our health, our family. Now, the life we had known was gone forever..

My chest ached. Tears blurred my vision. It wasn't fair. It wasn't right.

The part of me that had remained silent for so long, the part that remembered our life before the aneurysm, asserted itself. "You needn't go far," it said. "The next town over has a great bed and breakfast. All you need is a quiet room, a good book and one good night's sleep."

Drained and desperate, I gave in. The phone was in my hand. I nearly called Phil. I would have, if it wasn't for the guilt.

"How can you even think of abandoning your family?" I remember thinking. "Phil can't do it alone, not so soon after losing his brother. Liz puts on a brave face, but she's the one who found Elena. She needs to know it's not her fault. And what about Sammi? Ever time you leave the house she cries."

So it went, day after day, month after month. I fantasized about escape. My guilt devoured me. Until one day I stopped being so hard on myself.

I wish I could point to the one thing that lifted the guilt. I suppose the passage of time helped, as it often does. And there was the fact that as Elena grew stronger, I had more uninterrupted time to sleep, and process our passage through hell and back again. I can't give credit to any one reason; though I suspect the company of parents of special needs children had a heavy hand in it.

The details of their war stories differed from mine, but most, if not all of us, had arrived in the trenches in much the same way.

One day, one moment, all was well, normal. Predictable. Then all at once the world tipped sideways. Time slowed, suspended, held us hostage. In that moment, in that space, without asking permission, the illness, accident or circumstance stripped away our old lives, leaving our children forever and fundamentally changed.

The insights these parents spoke about revealed a universal truth. Raising children is hard enough. Raising children with special needs is damn near impossible at times. What's more, feeling trapped (and needing to escape) is not only normal, it's expected.

Once I let go of my guilt, I began the much-needed (and overdue) journey toward my own healing. All was well for a time. We moved Elena's bedroom downstairs because she could no longer safely navigate stairs on her own. We set up a baby monitor in our room so we could respond at a moment's notice when she needed us. Phil returned to work full time. My writing life took a backseat to Elena's recovery.

One week blurred into another. Elena's progress was slow going and unpredictable. Some days, she succeeded in dressing herself. Others, she struggled to snap her pants. As the months unfolded into years, it became clear Elena would never fully regain what she had lost physically or mentally.

An array of conflicting emotions took hold. Relief. Exhaustion. Elation. Gratitude. Resignation. Anger. Fear. My moods seesawed; I could never predict what would set me off. Elena's rigorous recovery schedule left little time for introspection.

I muscled through my days, attempting to keep up with the ever-growing clutter in my house, trying my best to be everything to everybody. Until one day, I had no choice but to look inward.

A day of firsts was to blame. First trip back to the hospital where Elena had spent three months fighting for her life. First time packing up for such a long trip. First time going it alone without Phil. First time loading and unloading Elena's wheelchair, finding a place to park, transporting her there and back again, and first time forcing my sleep-deprived brain to focus long enough to process what the physicians had to say about Elena.

The effort left me so exhausted I burst into tears the moment Phil returned home that evening.

I had no labels for what I was feeling when Phil pulled me into his arms that night, but this much I knew; if I was to be any good to my family in the coming months, I needed to understand what was happening to me.

One Sunday not long after the breakdown as our pastor launched into a sermon about life and love, and death and rebirth, I made the connection I needed.

I was in mourning for the loss of the Elena we once knew, for the loss of my identity outside of care-giving, and for the hard road we parents of special-needs children must travel. I needed to find a way to work through my grief. But how does a parent mourn the loss of a child—what they were and what they could have been?

The old Elena was much like every other nine year-old, except for the fact that she was very small for her age because of a rare form of dwarfism. She biked, played tag, made play dates, stayed up late at night reading books and giggling under the covers with her sister. When first home from the hospital, the new Elena was too weak to stand more than a minute at a time. In addition, she required frequent naps, used a wheelchair, and needed assistance with bathing, dressing, and spelling her name.

Saying goodbye to my bright, vivacious little girl felt like a betrayal. And more importantly, like I was giving up. I buried myself in Elena's recovery, determined to do everything I could to restore her.

In the end, Elena was the one who convinced me to let go.

While looking at an old photo album one day, Elena sat mesmerized by a picture taken when she was two. She was dressed in a green velvet dress, seated with her cousins on her great grandma's couch, her almond eyes grinning, her skinning legs dangling.

She smoothed her hand over the picture then looked up at me. "I'm not wearing a brace in this picture," she said.

Elena has worn a leg brace ever since her post-operative stroke left her leg permanently weakened. "No, you're not," I said.

"Hmmm."

I waited, not sure where she was headed.

"I look happy in this picture."

"Yes, you were."

She studied the picture once again. "You know what?"

"What?"

"I'm happy now, too….just like her."

From that day forward, I took Elena's lead. She had accepted who she was. Why couldn't I?

Elena's come a long way in five years. She's graduated from wheelchair to walker to cane. Her illnesses have decreased in number. She's well enough to last the whole day in school.

I've come a long way, too. I still wallow now and again, but when I catch myself doing so, it doesn't take much to lighten my mood. I need only seek out Elena. Her laugh brings me back, and the joy she takes in the simplest of everyday things—an afternoon tea, a manicure, a good fart joke, a game of Star Wars Monopoly, a Three Stooges episode.

At times like these, I'm reminded of what really matters — life, home, family, and loving Elena.

Tomorrow Will Come

Heide AW Kaminski

My son is sound asleep. My eyes are burning and my throat is sore. I feel like I am sitting at the bottom of an abyss with no rope to pull me out or hang myself with.

I am only human. I am an older mother and single to boot. I feel that I have reached the end of my rope. I don't want to be his mother anymore, I think. At the same time I am terrified for thinking this way, because you never know how the universe might respond to what you are asking for. I am ashamed. I gave birth to this child. My body nourished his for nine months and then my weak and aging body worked hard to keep nourishing the child even more. Physically, emotionally, spiritually.

I can't do it anymore, but I have to. I am my son's only hope. His father says, "He's just a boy," scoffing at the diagnosis of ADHD. I don't even send my son's medicine with him to his dads, because I think his dad would rather grind it up and sniff it than to give it to our son.

I came close today. I came close to calling the court and telling them to take my child. I am crying as I write this, because I am not the kind of mother who gives up on her child. I didn't give up during the first four years of his life, before he was diagnosed and medicated.

I was a zombie as I dragged my child into that office that eventually provided our family with the much-needed treatment for our son. I hadn't slept a single night since he was born. I didn't give up on him then. But I came close.

I begged and begged to have him tested for ADHD. Since he was only four, most everyone I saw was unwilling to go in that direction.

His first two years in school were filled with calls from the school until we finally found the correct meds. Then, finally, the news came that he was doing well. Which, in our case, meant no behavior problems.

As I write this, it is now the end of summer and he will be starting third grade soon. And, it's back. He is rude to everyone, including me, he doesn't ask, he demands. He is angry and not interested in any type of affection.

We went to the store. We had to leave, because he stomped around, knocking all the clothes off the racks. I have never spanked my child. But today, I certainly felt like whipping him. Right there in the store.

I was ready to call the court and tell them to take him away. I need to breathe, I am suffocating. I am suffocating with trying to teach my son how to be a nice child. God, I am not even asking so much. Look at someone's face and say thank you? Treat me like a human being, not like a slave on a pirate ship. Please talk like a normal person and do not grunt. Please go to sleep at bedtime and eat dinner before 10 p.m. Please be nice to the babysitter so she will come back tomorrow.

But I can't. I can't call the court, because if I do, he will have to go live with his father. He won't eat normal meals. He won't change his clothes or brush his teeth or comb his hair. But, worst of all, he won't get his meds and will get kicked out of school. He'll turn into a pothead before he is a teenager.

I have to go to bed and take advantage of the fact that he is sleeping right now. I have to rest.I will have to face a new tomorrow and I can't give up. One day, he will be better. One day he might just function fine without my constant guidance and protection.

I have to hang in there for him until that day. I know it will come. I know, because I have ADHD too and I know my mother sat in that same abyss with no rope to climb up on or to hang herself with. My mom gave up on me, but I never gave up on myself. And now I can't give up on my son. I know that beyond the ADHD driven anger is a fragile little boy begging me not to give up. I won't.

Off to See the Wizard

Marla Davishoff

As I wait on hold, listening to the elevator music, the knots in my stomach tighten. "How soon can we get an appointment?" I wonder, worrying the next available opening will be on a day my husband, Craig, can't take off from work. "We just had a cancellation a week from Thursday," the receptionist offers after hearing my discouragement about having to wait three months to get in. "Perfect!" I tell her, as my mind scrambles to recite all the necessary information they will need before an evaluation. Although I have done this almost a dozen times before in the past seven years, this time is going to be different. I am finally going to get concrete directions to help me navigate through the jungle of raising my second special needs son. This time I am going to do it right.

Sitting in the waiting room, I have some uninterrupted time to review all the forms that various therapists, teachers, and doctors have filled out to prepare our newest specialist for leading the way. "This is amazing," I say to Craig, as the pile seemingly reveals for the first time how many different diagnoses Bennett has been given over the years, including two congenital birth defects and a scattering of developmental delays. We discovered this specialist after insisting that one piece of the puzzle was still missing; something to tie this all together, to give it one name. After feeling the weight of the folder containing Bennett's medical information, I am certain we have finally made it to the right office. My quest for a unifying diagnosis that will lead to a treatment plan, and consequently a cure, will soon be fulfilled.

"The doctor is ready to see you," the receptionist calls as I jump out of my seat a step ahead of Craig. I feel a bit like Dorothy from the Wizard of Oz: the corridor leading to his office is my yellow brick road. After introductions and a brief review of our history, we sit down together, without my son, to talk about his case.

About fifteen minutes into our scheduled two hour appointment I suddenly realize this doctor is no wizard. In fact, he clearly isn't going to tell us anything we don't already know. "You are both already doing everything you can for Bennett," the doctor rather quickly assures us. Later, Craig tells me that he felt complimented; I felt patronized. I wanted something more. I had hoped this doctor held the secret key to opening the door to cure my son. However, I should have known better. After all, I was a psychotherapist before I had children and was often asked by my patients if there were any other way that I could help them feel better sooner. My standard response was "if I had a magic wand that would help people feel better I would be selling magic wands and instead of counseling families." It is obvious this doctor has no magic wands.

My husband and I sit patiently for the remainder of our appointment (Craig dozes off on only one occasion), thank the doctor for his time, shake hands, and leave. On our way to the elevator, Craig wonders out loud, "you think you know more than him, don't you?" He read my mind. The truth is, I don't want to know more than him, but secretly I know I do.

After being the mother of two special needs kids for seven years, I feel that I can pull rank and challenge the opinions of other professionals. I attend the same conferences, read the same books, and network with the same people. Even with all of this information at my disposal, it is through living and caring for them that I have gained my expertise. No expert can tell me how to explain to my son why invitations for play dates aren't reciprocated. No expert can explain to him why some members of our family are impatient with his stuttering or roll their eyes when he chews on his shirt.

It isn't only me who believes I know more than some of the professionals, but also Bennett, who is unusually insightful about his disabilities. I will never forget when Bennett asked me if he could stay home from a gymnastics themed birthday party that one of his friends was having. "I am bad at gymnastics," he told me with more certainty than is usually expected of a three and a half year-old. Although this was tough to hear, I was proud that he was honest to me and to himself about his limitations.

I am also amazed to watch my children adjust socially to being different. They seem to naturally surround themselves with a group of friends who understand their behaviors and issues. Bennett recently asked me if everybody's family goes to occupational and speech therapy. "No," I explained to him, "just most of the families we know." My husband and I have been fortunate enough to become friends with the parents of our children's friends as well. When we go out together our children may not seem normal to other people, but they are normal to each other. For that I am grateful.

The great wizard didn't tell me anything that I didn't already know. He just reinforced the fact that I need to believe in my instincts and intuitions. After all, becoming a parent has robbed me of my confidence more than I ever could have expected. I imagine that parent's of typical kids struggle with knowing what is best for their children too, but when I am constantly reminded that the hand I am playing involves higher stakes, I am especially careful about the risks. I forget how good my intuition is. I forget that I can't cure my boys but only can help them cope with their disability. I forget that the ruby red slippers were probably in my bag all along.

"Are you disappointed?" my husband asks as we drive home from the evaluation. "Not really," I tell him, "I am doing the best I can with our boys." I smile silently during the rest of the ride but as we pull into our driveway, I finally muster up the confidence to add "and I am beginning to realize that, just maybe, I am already doing it right."

Stealth

Swathi Avasthi

The morning light is blooming in the window; it's time for my eight year-old son, Nicholas, to stumble into the bedroom I share with his four year-old sister, Isabel, and crawl into my bed. From next door, I hear him swooshing down the slide that bridges his bunk bed to the floor and I feel the thump of his feet against the hardwood floor.

Isabel isn't awake yet. Our summertime rule: we don't wake each other up. When he comes to the door and peers in, I try to wave him off, but my motion doesn't stop him.

"Not yet," I whisper.
"Why not?" He says, full volume.

"Isabel is still asleep," I whisper again, trying to subtly remind him. But I know better: subtlety is lost on him, a child whose disorders prevent him from properly interpreting physical or social cues.

"FINE. NOW YOU'LL NEVER LET ME SNUGGLE WITH YOU AGAIN!"

He storms out of the room and slams the door. I clench my teeth and breathe slowly, not because of the explosion, but because he's woken up Isabel. Now, I'll have two fragile children to contend with all day. I believe it's unusual for an eight year-old to throw three tantrums in an hour but not that unusual for my eight year-old. For us, it's just an indication that we're in for another rough day.

I roll over to gather up my daughter. She is staring at the door and says, "It's okay, Mommy. It's not Nicholas' fault, it's mine."

Who is the forgotten child in my household? The one who received occupational therapy, physical therapy, an extra year in private kindergarten and reading tutoring? The one who has been tested so often that nobody worries at the appearance of another expert? Or is it the one who has been dragged along to tests, therapies, and tutors? The one who has been screamed at by her brother over and over? The one who defends her brother when I defend her?

There is so much literature available to me as a mother. I read three bookshelves' worth of parenting books and still wondered why none of them seemed to pertain to my child.

I started reading books on gifted children since Nicholas tested in the 99th percentile on three different intelligence tests. Those had limited use. And when Nicholas was diagnosed, I filled up another bookshelf with ADHD and Sensory Integration Dysfunction books. Even though I'm still wondering if anyone gets my child, I can find support groups, doctors, therapies, and friends. But what is available for my daughter?

We waited three years from the time we suspected there was a problem until he was six (old enough for a diagnosis), to try to name what was different about him, to shed some light and give us strategies. But when he was diagnosed, theNeuropsych told me that his disorder is not exactly ADHD and not exactly NVLD (non-verbal learning disability). It isn't in DSM IV (the mental health professional's bible that defines all recognized mental disorders) and isn't coming out in DSM V. So, she said, since he fits best into the ADHD box, we'll put him there. When ADHD medication made so little difference that his teacher couldn't tell when he was taking it, our confidence in the label eroded further. He is beset with an unnamed disorder. His behavior, the screaming and irrational conclusions, stems from the friction between what he can understand and what he can accomplish.

Explaining to my daughter that it's not her fault that he shouts at her is easy in theory.

"Honey," I say, "You didn't do anything wrong. You were asleep." When that doesn't work, I try, "Do you climb into Nicholas' throat and make him scream at you? It's <u>his</u> choice."

But she doesn't believe me, and each time he yells at her, I end up having the same talk with her. For her, it's more comfortable to believe that she is at fault than that someone she idolizes is dysfunctional.

So, in addition to my concern for my son, I'm left with worry for her. What lessons is she learning? What will she do in fifteen years when her boyfriend shouts at her? Will she cover for him, think it's her fault, and enable him to yell more? And where will that lead?

Suddenly, I'm back five years ago, when I watched Nicholas start to slip from me as the disorder swallowed up my son. Where did that promising, happy child go? And what has this unnamed disorder left me with?

Now, it's taking my daughter, too. Not the same way it took my son from me, no. Will I have to grieve for her in a different way that is so subtle, I cannot describe it, cannot give it a name?

***

Maria Montessori says that as parents, we are our child's first teachers. But that's only true for the first-born. After that, children learn from their siblings first.

A few days ago, a month before her fifth birthday, I found Isabel with her fingers propped up, trying to snap. I showed her how to do it and folded her last two fingers down.

She looked at me patronizingly and said, "I'll ask Nicholas to teach me how to snap. He's teaching me how to be an eight year-old."

Obviously not something I had mastered.

Last year, Nicholas performed in a school play. Afterward, the audience was allowed to ask questions. Isabel raised her hand, and when she was called on, she said, "I want to ask a question, but can only Nicholas answer?"

She has chosen her first teacher, and it is not me.

***

Isabel was quick to her feet. At six months, when most kids are dribbling from their juice cups, she would hold her father's fingers and toddle about, dribbling a soccer ball around the living room. She began to walk when she was seven months-old and was running before she was one. Like her father, who ran track in college and is preparing for a marathon now, she had an easy, natural stride and a speed that defied her age. She started taking gymnastics when she was two. Being petite and strong, it seemed she would go far, maybe even farther than I wanted.

Her brother is not athletic. In addition to a hesitant ADHD diagnosis, he has a reading disorder and coordination problems. When he was four, he would flop over in his booster seat while eating. Even today, two years after physical therapy and thousands of push-ups, I still need to tell him to sit up instead of crumpling over his seatbelt in the car. At six, his weak muscles showed themselves when he ran. He leaned so far forward that his chest was parallel to the ground, making his back into a tabletop. At seven, he had learned to straighten up, but stuck his elbows out and bent dramatically at the waist with each stride.

Isabel was three then, watching him run with pleasure, if not coordination. In vast admiration, her elbows came out, her waist started to turn, and her natural stride was shortened. Now that she is four, she still gets pleasure from physical activity, but she is no longer on the fast track in gymnastics. Not a tragedy, to be sure. In a certain way, not even something to complain about. But, I wonder, what could she do without his disorder?

Granted, he teaches her many good things. He has caution; she has none. He has a detail-oriented mind and rule-oriented play; she changes the rules every time they don't suit her. Granted, she has taught him as well. Where he has frowns and anger, she has smiles and laughter. With determined joy, she has reached into the abyss and brought back my happy son. Overall, they are a great pair.

I can rationalize; I can make lemonade; I can see the strengths in differences. But on a fundamental level, I will always hate this disorder that has siphoned off potential from both of my children.

Years ago, I learned that I'll never know who he would be without this disorder pressing on him — an elephant sitting on his tabletop back while he runs. And now, I've come to see that I'll never know who she could be either. Five years after we began to suspect that an unnamed disorder was stealing from my son, and then from my daughter, I am finally able to corner it, shine a light on it, and call it by its name: Thief.

Not Even Ice Cream

Jennifer Bailey

Perhaps it was after a year of being covered in vomit an average of four times a day that I realized my life is not exactly normal. You might think having to feed your child via g-tube would be blunt enough to shock you into reality, but no. I think sometimes parents are the greatest optimists, hoping that "this to will pass" and someday "we will overcome." Three and a half years later, my son still is not eating and we have run out of specialists who even pretend to know what we are facing and how to address it.

Looking at my son, you may not immediately realize that he has had so many medical challenges and surgeries. Clothes cover a lot. So does cuteness. He has exceptional features, a kind of glowy strawberry-blond hair, and thoughtful eyes that belie the perseverative behaviors and constant anxiety he faces.

This "attractive bias" is found even in my own friends and family who at times seem to forget the struggles he faces. Their casual comments, "oh, right. I forgot he was still on a g-tube" isolate me and leave the difficulties of hooking him up to a feeding pump every day unacknowledged. It is so easy to assume that even people with special needs (especially if they don't have any obvious, external assistive-equipment) can at least eat, breathe, and sleep. My son, Ethan, does not choose to eat and has been on a prolonged hunger strike since he turned one.

The amount of well-intentioned but uninformed advice sometimes makes me sarcastic. I cannot tell you how many times after telling someone that Ethan does not eat any food they have exclaimed "not even ice cream?" in scandalized tones. When explaining that Ethan has sensory issues that complicate chewing and swallowing, some rocket-science genius suggested we try chewing gum. Why hadn't I (and the team of feeding specialists) thought of that? I contemplated sitting on Ethan for an hour trying to pry his mouth open.

My husband and I walk into restaurants with Ethan and blithely order only two meals for ourselves. When the waiter suggest a child's menu, it is often difficult to explain that he does not eat. Often we do takeout, to avoid the stares if he starts screaming or banging on the table. Often we have been offered treats such as cookies for Ethan who barely glances at the offered food. To avoid controversy, I mumble thanks and quickly stuff the food in my bag knowing he will never look at it, let alone touch it. Once a cashier at a Thai restaurant insisted Ethan sample something she was offering. I tried to explain that he did not eat, but perhaps a slight language barrier led to confusion. I finally lifted his shirt to indicate his g-tube and the shocked look on the woman's face made me hurriedly exit the restaurant to relieve her discomfort. Though I felt badly, I giggled wickedly the whole way home.

It's a Mad, Mad World

Heather Ristau

"Why can't you listen to me?!" I yelled again, mere inches from his face. You would think that by now I would realize the futility of raising my voice to get his attention. But the constant fluctuation of his moods and the intensity of his own anger often causes mine to grow and spill out into hot, loud, angry words that do nothing more than echo off the walls and bounce back into my heart. They mock me with every resonation, announcing to my very soul that I have let him down again by neglecting to stay calm through his very difficult storms.

Samuel is only four years-old and yet has the power to elicit responses from me that I didn't even know I was capable of. He has been diagnosed with several issues from ADHD to mood disorders but what that translates into for our daily life is a little boy who has a very hard time keeping his cool in the face of disappointment or challenge. His moods can change from overly sad, to awkwardly happy, to violently angry within the span of a few hours. I have been living with these moods for several years now, watching them grow and develop, and you would think that I would have learned how to properly respond. I do have to admit, that things are better than they used to be, and I am often able to lovingly soothe him, but some days when I am exhausted from riding the mood roller coaster, my weakness rises to the surface and my anger rears its own ugly head to join in the chaos.

I never knew how all-consuming and difficult motherhood could be. I was a great babysitter and spent all my free time with children. Teaching them, playing with them, loving them, spending time with them. The big difference was that I wasn't responsible for training them, protecting them, and raising them to be confident and productive adults. That small difference has shaken me to my core and left me a little angry at the secret of motherhood that no one seems to be sharing. Motherhood is vastly different than we all dreamed it would be. Daily, I look around and wonder what in the world it was that I actually accomplished today. I find myself jealous of my husband and working mothers, not because I really want a job, but because they can formulate a to-do list and actually check things off that don't slide back on sometime during the hours of the day. I'm aware that raising my sons is a powerful contribution to the world at large and that the way I spend my hours and days will eventually add up to the very fiber of their childhood. I think I just feel alone. I think that many of us feel alone. Our husbands don't understand this sentiment as we are surrounded daily by little people, but these are people who we are molding for the world not people that are in existence to be our partners in life. And so out of desperation and much selfish desire, I turn to God.

I direct much of my frustration His way, and in the next breath I beg Him to make my son all better. I have found that the complexities of my emotions regarding motherhood are only safe between us. It seems as though no one can fully comprehend what happens on those days we are alone at home and I don't know how to soothe my raging son. So I cry to the one person who I know won't condemn me, reject me, reprimand me or try to give empty advice. I have decided to believe through personal experience that the one who promises to love does just that. And that love is what enables me to continue loving Samuel. I draw from it, I rely on it, I gather up remnants of hope from this love. This love is what has protected me from myself and enabled me to be angry but not to live as an angry person. It has helped me to be able to question my ability as Samuel's mother and yet never give up. It has assured me that no matter how many times I have screwed up in the past that tomorrow is fresh and offers me new mercies for my circumstance. I want to celebrate that.

I have been shocked at the intensity of anger I have experienced. I didn't see it as anger for a long time, and had a hard time admitting that it was the crux of my problem. However as Samuel grew and his rages and depressed times became more mature and more complicated, I realized just how angry I was. Sadly, I directed this anger at him more times that I would like to remember. Its amazing to me how someone so beautiful, someone who needs me so much and trusts me implicitly can bring out anger in me that seemed to boil up out of my belly and explode into the safety of his childhood atmosphere with such power. Having a child who won't obey simple commands such as "go get dressed now" can be a frustrating experience, but having a child who looks you square in the eye and says "no, I hate you, you stupid mommy" while trying to punch you in your pregnant belly is enough to send most people over the edge. When that confusion on his face looks like disobedience and he stands looking up at me with his blinking, defiant eyes I find myself wanting to squeeze his face with my hands until a tooth shoots out at me. The violent frustration I feel is frightening and raw and hurls me into the land of mommy guilt where the air is so thick with regret I can barely breathe. I am relieved to say that I have not abused him. I am ashamed to say that I have done more than I ever thought I was capable of. I have jerked his arm, screamed in his face, pushed him too harshly into bed, told him to shut up, thrown things in the room, kicked a hole in the wall, punched my bed with abandon, slammed things around, and yelled some more. The only thing that has kept me from shoving my fist through his chest has been knowing how much I truly do adore him, and while the split second of physical release may feel good, I know enough to know, that the pain I would experience afterward would not be the taste of success.

Right now, mornings are the worst. We need to get to his Pre-K class by 8:00 am. He isn't an easy child to motivate and prefers to do things on his own time. My agenda of getting him fed, dressed and out the door couldn't be less important to him. I yell, I make threats to take away video games, or after school treats, and he just stares at me, cocking his head to one side as though trying to get a better understanding of his raving mother and her annoyingly loud voice. Somehow, we manage to make it to the school, and I try my best to motivate him to get out of the car. He cries that he only wants to be with me, the best mommy in the world, and I cringe with guilt. The director sees us in the parking lot for five, ten, fifteen minutes and comes out to try and help me convince him, yet again, to go into his classroom. Eventually he does, and I drive my emotionally tired self home to spend some unchallenged hours with my other son and wait for the return of excitement.

I watch mothers around me and wonder if any of them ever get mad the way that I do. I'm especially intrigued with moms who have kids with struggles and wonder how much guilt they are carrying around in their back pockets. I silently scold myself for not being mature enough to handle the episodes more lovingly, with more peace and more mercy. I promise myself that I won't yell again. We have a special moment together when his brain is working the way it was designed to and he lavishes kisses and sweet nothings on me. I am his sole obsession. I brush back his sun-streaked hair and look into his eyes that seem to be colored from crushed blueberries and marvel that this charming boy can feel so out of control. I tell him I love him. I assure him that even when I'm angry that I still love and adore him. I feel hopeful again. I begin to think that it's all been in my head and we won't ever go through any episodes again. Maybe he's outgrown it! Just look at him! He's adorable. And then, just as I begin to breathe, and can smile at him and believe myself of all the promises I have made, it is once again the morning.

Of Course I Did

Andrea Harris

After hugging William goodbye, I joined the group of nervous mothers huddled by the classroom door. I managed not to cry for exactly thirty seconds, right up until the moment when he put away his "Blue's Clues" backpack. Something about the efficient way he hung the backpack on the metal hook and then calmly walked away made me feel as if I, too, was being "put away." One of the other mothers handed me a tissue and smiled. I remember being amazed at the more experienced moms who quickly kissed their younger children goodbye and then walked away without a backward glance. How did they do it? Several of us "first-timers" stood there in quiet empathy for several minutes after class had started, unwilling to turn away. We were waiting for some sign that our kids would be okay, yet simultaneously hoping for a last desperate look from them that would confirm how much they still needed us. My head knew that William would be just fine; my heart, however, was having trouble accepting that my son would be just fine *without* me.

Four years later, I stood in a different hallway outside another door and watched my younger son Joshua walk into his kindergarten classroom for the first time. This time, I was too scared to cry. It took every ounce of strength I had not to march into the room, take every single kid aside, and explain to them that Joshua was a little different, that his brain worked a little differently than their brains. I would have been perfectly willing to get down on both knees and beg them to be nice to him, not to make fun of him, to try to understand. His teacher must have seen the look on my face because she came over to me and reassured me that he would be fine. There would be an aide with him at all times; her own son had a learning disability. I nodded and tried to smile, but I spent the rest of that day staring at the clock, waiting for the phone call that would make me grab my keys and rush back to the school.

When Josh was with me, I could keep him safe. I could explain to everyone else why he acted the way he did. I was really good at the explanations. He was happy at home. At home we honored his routines and respected his obsessions. We didn't expect him to act like everyone else. Even when he had attended the preschool for kids with disabilities, I had not worried. There, *he* was the "normal" one. The other children had much more obvious physical disabilities. Joshua's high-functioning autism has always allowed for a wide range of behaviors and skills. On a good day, involved in the right activity, he could seem like every other kid his age. But now that Josh would be surrounded all day, five days a week, by kids without any "special needs," the autism would be impossible to hide.

I was terrified that my beautiful son would have no friends, that the other kids would make fun of him, that the teachers would resent him. I worried that he would be labeled the "weird kid." My worries did not go away as the school year went on. I met regularly with his teacher, quizzing her about Joshua's interactions with the other kids. Although she admitted that he always played by himself, she assured me that no one was teasing him. I was comforted by her insistence that Joshua's artistic ability helped the other kids accept him. She told me that sometimes the other children would line up just to ask Josh to draw something for them. His talent, like his teacher, helped protect him. By the end of the school year I had managed to replace the mental image of my child playing alone during recess with the image of my son happily drawing dinosaurs for a line of eager classmates.

Then one day, I opened Joshua's homework folder to find an invitation to the annual musical performance. He had mentioned nothing about the performance, and, when I questioned him about it, all he said was that he didn't like music class. As the date for the performance approached, I considered several alternatives. I considered keeping him home that day, calling the office and saying he was sick. Even worse, *I* considered not going. I was a coward. I couldn't bear the thought of seeing my son become a public spectacle, of seeing the differences between him and the other kids made so blatantly obvious in front of a crowd of people. It wasn't the fear of what my child would do that made me want to stay at home; it was the fear of what the *other* people would do. It was the fear of drowning in the realization that I could not protect my child from the world any more, that I could not take every single person aside and explain my son to them. I worried that even if I did explain things to them, some people would still never like Joshua or try to understand. At some point, all parents have to accept that they cannot protect their kids; for many parents of children with disabilities, however, this heart-tearing realization is not softened by the thought that our children may fit in, may not need our protection, may actually be able to protect themselves.

The morning of the music performance, I made sure that Joshua looked especially nice. I carefully combed his hair and checked twice to make sure that he had not replaced the socks that matched his shirt with his favorite lime green pair. When I dropped him off at

school, I told him that I would see him later at the music performance and asked him as calmly as possible to please do whatever the
music teacher asked him to do. As I drove away, I was filled with
shame; I had wanted so badly to tell him just to try to be like everyone else, to fit in, just for today, just for this one performance.

When I arrived at the music room that afternoon, only a few seats
were left. It seemed like every kid in Joshua's class had two parents
and at least two, sometimes four, grandparents in attendance. I had
invited my parents, but they both still worked during the day. Joshua
had not seen his father since the divorce four years ago. As I sat there
listening to the excited conversations of all the proud parents and
grandparents, I had never felt more alone. Then, when the kids filed
in, and I watched my son walk slowly into the room in his place at
the end of the line, I realized that at least one other person felt as
alone as I did.

All the other kids were waving excitedly at their family members, but
Josh was staring at the floor. I wanted to yell to him, tell him that I
was there, but the words wouldn't come out. Then, he must have
remembered that I had said I would be there, because he looked up
expectantly and began scanning the crowd. Although I was only a few
feet away, it seemed to take him forever to recognize the furiously
waving woman in the third row as his mother. He smiled at me and
raised his hand in a half-wave; then he was gone, disappearing at the
end of the second row behind his classmates. His aide stood off to the
side, poised to jump in when needed.

As the crowd quieted, the prayer in my head grew louder: "Please let
Josh make it through this thing without doing anything too weird.
Please let Josh make it through this thing without doing anything too

weird." Over and over I repeated this plea, as if it were some powerful mantra. My biggest fear was that he would suddenly decide to remove some article of clothing that was bothering him or that he would randomly break into his pterodactyl imitation. But, as the song began, and I strained my head to see Josh behind the other kids, I realized that my mantra had not worked. Josh was having one of those days when his autism decides to put on bells and do a little jig.

As the other kids sang, my son stared down at the floor and picked at his fingers. At his feet, a tiny pile of pieces of nails and skin began to grow. The other parents were taking pictures of their kids singing and smiling. I had not even thought to bring a camera. I had a camera in my phone, though, and I wanted nothing more at that moment then to be able to call out "Josh!" and then snap a picture of him. Kids *should* have pictures of their first school performance in the family photo album. Joshua's brother William had pictures of *his* first performance.

I held my camera in the air with one hand, waving the other. The woman next to me smiled sympathetically. Josh wouldn't even look up. His gaze was fixated on his hand. He seemed unaware that everyone around him was singing and making motions with their arms. I closed my phone and stopped waving.

After two songs, the kids partnered for the square dancing portion of the performance. I looked down at my feet, afraid to watch. Joshua had not been obvious stuck in the back row during the first two songs, but dancing with a partner was something else. As the music started, I forced myself to look up. Josh's partner was a pretty little girl who had been very carefully dressed for this special occasion. Josh, of course, refused to move, let alone dance. I watched in anguish as the little girl tried in vain to pull him across the floor. His feet were rooted; his eyes still fixated on his hand.

At first, it was kind of funny, and some of the parents tittered, but, as the girl got more and more upset, the school aide stepped in. I could see the girl's parents out of the corner of my eye. The father was frowning, and the mother was alternately lowering and raising her camera, trying to encourage her daughter with her smile. When she turned to say something to her husband, I looked away. From the look in her eyes, I knew what she was going to say: "Why did our daughter have to get stuck with the weird kid?" Four years ago, if William had been stuck with a little girl who refused to move, I probably would have thought the same thing.

The rest of the performance was a blur, seen through the tears that I refused to let fall. Josh had been led off the dance floor by the aide, and the little girl who had been his partner stood beside him, crying. Now that my fears had come true, I was angry at everyone. Angry with the music teacher that Joshua had been forced to participate in a public performance. Angry with the little girl's parents for acting like square dancing was the biggest event in their daughter's life. Angry with everyone who looked at my child like there was something wrong with him because he didn't dance and smile on cue. Angry most of all, though, with myself for even considering not coming. I almost didn't hear the sound of the applause, I was so intent on trying to get Joshua to look up so that I could smile at him and let him know that everything was okay.

After the performance was over, the audience was invited back to the classroom. I stood at the door and watched the children welcome their proud parents and grandparents. The parents of Joshua's partner were comforting her; Joshua's teacher was making explanations. Everyone else was acting like nothing had happened, but I could feel their eyes on me as I made my way to Joshua's desk. He looked up from the picture he was drawing and smiled at me. "You came," he said. "Of course, I did," I told him as I smiled back.

Details

Lorena Smith

I am on my hands and knees, trying desperately to wipe up the water that has overflowed from the bathtub before I incur even more water damage expenses. The water has run into the closet and all the clothes I've dumped on the floor because I was too tired to put them away are soaked. The carpet in my bedroom squelches when I walk on it.

While I was downstairs vacuuming the contents of an entire box of corn flakes off the kitchen floor, the living room floor and every-where else, my son started the bathwater and hopped in fully clothed, watching the water flow from the tap into the bath, flowing, flowing, flowing....

I know he's trying to calm himself from the obvious distress I showed when I saw the cereal on the floor everywhere. I couldn't help it. I had already mopped up a gallon of milk that he had tried to serve himself, ignoring the cup of milk I always keep in the fridge for him.

I hear a crash from downstairs. I know it's the Christmas tree. I knew I shouldn't have bought one, but my daughter so wanted a normal Christmas. I knew it was only a matter of time till he got fascinated with the ornaments and pulled it down.

By now, I am so weary and so disheartened that I want to lie down in the bath myself and never get up.

I am afraid to go downstairs and see what chaos awaits me. Sure enough, the Christmas tree lies on its side. The ornaments are smashed into a thousand pieces. The dry pine needles have exploded onto every conceivable surface.

I want to scream. And then I see JJ. He is standing in the corner naked. He has a huge smile, pure bliss on his face. He is glowing. He has draped himself in the shining Christmas lights. As I look at him, I unexpectedly want to giggle. He gives me a huge smile, his eyes meeting mine as he imitates his favorite video. I. Am. That. HEEEEWWOOOOO!!!

As I gather my little glowing hero into my arm, I begin to think that a living, breathing Christmas tree is better than the dead one lying on the floor. Suddenly, he reaches out his chubby arms and gives me an unusual, huge, spontaneous hug.

Were outside trying to take a walk. I say trying because JJ doesn't feel like exercising today. He is flopping and falling and just generally making a fuss. Alex wants to get to the park and play and she is skipping ahead of us over the bridge. We get to the little wooden bridge over the creek and JJ will not move. He throws himself on his stomach over the edge, under the bars and stares down into the water. I cannot lift him or yell him into moving. His eyes stare unknowingly at me and then back at the water fascinated. I don't know what to do.

Alex comes back to see why we are taking so long to catch up to her and asks me what he is looking at. My mind is busy trying to figure out how to move him and make him walk. She throws herself down next to him, sticks her head under the railing and looks too.

"Oh, mom, look. Look," she says excitedly. So, I too, lie down on the bridge and stick my head under the railing. Thousands of tiny little fish are swimming in the water, their bodies gleaming Like an underwater rainbow. They look positively breathtaking.

Alex moves so she can lay her head right next to mine and JJ maneuvers so he can throw an arm around my head. We count colors while JJ gurgles and smiles and mumbles. "Look, JJ. Can you say Fish? Say Fish? Alex has heard this drill many times. Suddenly, he looks up at her and says, quite clearly, PISS.

She giggles with him until they are laughing out loud as all three of us watch the fish wiggle and shine their light on us. God is in the details.

Hostage

Sheila Webster-Heard

In a coma-like sleep, I could still hear Darius's string of high-pitched babbles in the next room. It sounded something like a ritualistic chant; bizarre, yet soothing. Everyday he woke up, sang his song and stared at the ceiling. This had become a normal part of our lives.

Little by little I parted my eyes to what I thought was a faint knocking at the door. Exhausted, I pushed the sheets to the side of the bed and yawned.

"Who could this be?"

It wasn't early in the morning, it was eleven a.m., but I had been up all night with Darius who was going through a bout of night terrors. A bad dream would often send him charging into our bedroom and because of the artery-bursting wailing accompanying him, our first thought was, "He must be in pain." However, after countless trips to urgent care and the emergency room revealed absolutely nothing, my husband and I were certain that nightmares were causing his disturbance. There was no way we would ever really know though. At two and a half years-old, Darius still couldn't talk, but boy could he scream. He would shriek for hours on end in his car seat, at the grocery store; even a slightly different route on the way home would get him going, "AAAAAAHHHHHHH!" he'd cry out hysterically.

I was completely out of ideas so I was elated when he and the birds outside got together for a whimsical duet at the crack of dawn. Darius' morning mantra continued to echo in my head as I opened the door. All of a sudden a force knocked me down, went into Darius's room and grabbed him.

After peeling myself off of the maroon carpet, the only thing I could think to do was go at it full force, put my hands around its arm and yank as hard as I could. I was determined to unlatch it from my child. I was so confident I could save Darius. I mean, before I even had children, I imagined every scenario possible, preparing myself for "stay away from stranger danger" and "say no to drugs" and "practice safe sex" talks. I was ready for everything. But I wasn't ready for Autism.

"He's mine," Autism said, slowly revealing its unsettling smile beneath a mask of stubbornness. It refused to let go and after many days and nights of tug-of-war, our unwelcome guest told me he would be staying for good. It said my life would be filled with angst as I watched my son fail to develop mentally. The simple things, this thing told me, my son would never be able to do.

"Forever a prisoner to me," it said.

And the screams, it said. I still had to bear those stabbing, agonizing screams continuing for hours at a time. As if that wasn't already too much to bear, Autism had been in my home before. Right before my very eyes it had already grabbed my older son, Douglas. But because it was so clever and I was so misinformed by a number of physicians, I didn't have a clue. As a result, valuable time was wasted and the more time passed, the more I realized I was losing precious pieces of my sons. Some of those pieces gone forever.

Autism told me it would impair my family life and it did just that. It seemed delighted it had affected us severely, but was disappointed that its presence had made all of us stronger and much closer. Unfortunately, there are still days when we are under Autism's command but never once have I given it total supremacy. It hangs onto Darius with a vengeance and my child's eyes say, "Please mommy don't give up on me." I won't.

Doctors have told me Darius will never lead a normal life. Some teachers have said   he will never talk and that he should be medicated. My response to them is, "you don't understand how powerful a cure love is."

Yes, our unwanted guest is still with us and everyday we learn to live with it. But lately it has gone missing for small periods of time and when it leaves, in its place remains a giggle, a kiss or even a word or two from Darius. Douglas is inspiring. He pushes forward with purpose and with every new achievement; Autism has had to step further into the background. Finally, we've come to a small agreement, Autism and me. I agree to continue to fight for my sons and Autism agrees to eventually, loosen its grip.

Knowing Henry

Susan Wagner

One morning, when I was eight weeks pregnant with our first baby, I told my husband, "We're having a boy."

I was certain about this, for no good reason. It was the first time I had felt anything approaching confidence about this pregnancy. We were walking down a little side street in Tacoma on our way to meet friends for breakfast and suddenly, I felt like I was really going to have a baby. A son. "We're having a boy." "Really?" he said. "Okay, then, I think it's a girl."

"No, I'm serious. The baby is a boy." "How do you know?" "I just know."

I am not the type of person who just *knows* things. I can count, on one hand, the number of times that I have correctly intuited anything. I prefer to be prepared, to be forewarned, to assess what all the possible outcomes are. I believe in intuition, but I don't typically find that I am able to make decisions solely on my gut feeling. I like to have a plan. I like to be certain about what I know.

My approach to motherhood went like this: I read about strategies for conception and the early signs of pregnancy. I read about what to eat and how to exercise. I read about how to manage stress and how to sleep better. When a year passed, and then two, and I was still not pregnant, I started reading about fertility testing and treatments, about the success rates of various procedures and the side effects of various drugs. I read about adoption, about the differences between social services adoptions and private adoptions. I learned the ins and outs of open adoption. When we finally confirmed—after four pee-on-the-stick pregnancy tests and two go-to-the-lab blood tests— that yes, I was really pregnant, I started reading about pregnancy and labor and delivery. At a friend's recommendation, I read up on the signs of premature labor, although I couldn't imagine not carrying to term. We chose a hospital with a Level Three NICU, although we were certain we wouldn't need it. Through all of this, I knew that I didn't really *know* anything, that I wouldn't really know what it was like to give birth, to be a mother, until it happened, but I was as prepared as I could be. I knew that the unknown was out there and I was ready for it.

But I *knew* that the baby was a boy. On the day our son was born, six weeks before his due date, weighing less than five pounds, the nurse announced, "It's a boy!" and I looked at my husband and said, "I told you."

"You were right," he said. We named the baby Henry Forsyth; Forsyth for my father and Henry for himself. He went directly from the delivery room to the NICU and stayed there for ten days. He struggled to breathe and was on and off a ventilator. He was on antibiotics for whatever infection it was that caused my water to break at 34 weeks. I went home less than 24 hours after the delivery because there was nothing I could do for my son, lying in his little plastic bed, tethered to a half dozen monitors. I started my life with this boy feeling like I was already failing him.

I brought a hospital-grade breast pump home with me and set it up in the nursery; I got up every three hours to pump. My day revolved around the pumping and the 25 minute drive to the hospital, where I went three times a day to sit with Henry and to deliver the tiny bits of breast milk I was expressing. The nurses would look at the tubes and say, very kindly, "Is this all?" It seemed like a lot of work for nothing, but when I would ask the nurses, they encouraged me to keep at it. "You need to rest and relax," one nurse told me. "And think of your baby when you pump. That will help your milk let down." When I thought of Henry I saw tubes and billirubin lights and the plastic box he lived in. Wade had the nurses show him how to take Henry out of the isolette, how to hold him, how to give him a bottle, but I was afraid to touch my son. I wasn't sure what I was supposed to do now that he was here. I thought I would know, but I didn't.

When Henry came home, I spent all my time caring for him. Every feeding took over an hour; Henry was a slow eater and had to be burped often. He spat up, every single time, all over me and the chair and the floor, which made me crazy. Didn't he know how hard it was to express that breast milk? Didn't he understand how little milk there was? After I fed him, I pumped, which took another 45 minutes and rarely yielded enough milk for an entire feeding. Because he was premature, we had strict orders to feed him every three hours to be sure he was eating enough. Later, when he was diagnosed with reflux, the specialist recommended that we continue feeding him every three hours to be sure his stomach wasn't too full. I did nearly all the feedings because Wade had to go to work. After each feeding, Henry would cry and cry and cry, probably from the reflux. I would fall asleep giving him his bottle or pumping. Often, I sobbed along with him because I didn't know what else I could do for him and I was so fucking tired that I couldn't even think straight.

I read a lot, anything I could find. I kept a tower of baby books on the table in the nursery and I would read while I pumped. One of these experts, I reasoned, would know the things I needed to know, would know about this baby who didn't seem to be like other babies. He wanted to be held all the time but he screamed bloody murder when we put him in the Baby Bjorn. He hated the jumpy swing but when we would put him in his bouncy seat, he would kick his legs and rock the seat until his bottom was bouncing off the floor. He refused a pacifier, preferring instead to suck on my finger. He didn't respond when I talked to him or sang to him or made faces at him, like all my books said to do, but he cried when I left the room or walked out of his sight. I didn't know what I was doing but I was clearly doing it wrong.

Everywhere we went, the park, the mall, I watched other women with their babies. I watched as babies Henry's age played with balls and sat in swings and waved at smiling grownups. At Gymboree, Henry would crawl away from the rest of the class and sit in front of the mirrored walls babbling to himself. He would wait until circle time started and the other babies were playing together on the parachute to climb on the equipment. He would cry if I walked away. I had hoped that Gymboree would be a way to meet other women, to pick their brains about how to do this mommy thing, but instead I spent each class following Henry around. I watched the other mommies and babies and I wondered how they knew what to do, how to play together. I wondered if I would ever know enough about my son to understand why he was so different.

By the time Henry was nine months-old, he had severe stranger anxiety. No matter who I left him with, he cried and cried, not just for two minutes or ten but until I came back, no matter how long that was. We never used babysitters because it was just too hard, on them and on Henry and on us.

One afternoon, on the way to a bridal shower, my mother-in-law said to me, "I wish I could help you more with Henry." "That's okay," I told her. "You're busy and Sheila needs your help more." My other sister-in-law had two babies and a husband who traveled a lot; I had one baby and a husband who came home for dinner every night. As much as I would have liked an afternoon to myself or an evening out with Wade, I didn't think I needed the help as much as Sheila did.

"No, that's not it," my mother-in-law said. "I don't think Henry would stay with me. I would keep him, but I don't think he would stay with me."

I wanted to argue with her, but I had just left Henry refusing to let Wade feed him, sobbing because I was not the one holding the bottle, trying to climb out of Wade's lap and follow me out of the house. I knew that my mother-in-law was right, that if I left Henry with her, he would be a wreck. I didn't know why this was or what to do about it, but I knew that somehow it was my fault.

Henry loved doors. He would spend entire afternoons opening and closing the cabinet doors in our kitchen, in my mother-in-law's kitchen and in the kitchens of my playgroup friends. He wasn't interested in what was in the cabinets, just the doors. We joked that he would grow up to be a doorman in a fancy apartment building.

When Henry was 14 months old, I went to Chicago for a long week-end. Wade stayed home with Henry and took him to a birthday party for our three year-old niece. While the other kids, played in the yard and ate pizza, Henry stayed in the kitchen, opening and closing the cabinets. "Didn't he go outside?" I asked Wade.

He shrugged. "He didn't want to. Besides, it was hot."

"But the other kids were outside, right? Sheila had games for them, and toys. Why didn't he go outside?" "I took him outside and he cried and wanted to go back in. All he wanted to do was play with the doors." Wade looked at me, frustrated. "It's *fine*," he said. "He's fine." But I was starting to know that he wasn't.

At two, Henry only knew 14 words, despite the fact that I read to him all the time, book after book, for hours during the day. He wasn't combining words to make sentences like "go car" or "go night night." Six weeks before our second baby was due, my pediatrician decided that it was entirely possible that Henry wasn't talking because he didn't have to, because I was always with him and knew what he wanted, because I let him not talk. She laid down the law: "You need to get him talking. When he wants something, make him ask for it. If he wants milk, make him say *milk*." That was in June; if Henry wasn't talking by August, we would need to have him evaluated by a speech pathologist, to determine if there was a larger problem.

That very day, we started insisting that he use his words. By the end of the day, he had said "up" and "down" and "chip" and "please." Three days later, Henry started asking for things and putting words together; two weeks later, he was talking in complete sentences. I wrote his words down on the calendar, eight or ten or sometimes fifteen new words each day, and breathed a sigh of relief. But now I was convinced that everything really was my fault and I needed to do a better job.

The summer Henry turned two, our second son, Charlie, was born. Henry had no interest in Charlie, not so much because Charlie was a baby but because Henry was completely obsessed with all things related to lawn mowing. His first real sentences were about mowing. "Daddy mow grass! Daddy mow now! I help Daddy mow!" He would meet Wade at the door every night and insist, "Daddy, are you going to mow the grass tonight?" He could identify weed eaters and edgers and various types of mowers. He would point out every lawn service truck we passed and would beg us to drive around the block to "look for guys mowing." His favorite outing was to Lowe's, where he would sit on the riding mowers and look at all the leaf blowers. For his second birthday, my father-in-law brought him a little pop mower. He spent his entire party pretending to mow the grass while the other kids played in the splash pool and rode in the plastic car and chased each other around. When everyone came inside to eat cake, he stayed in the yard, all alone, mowing. I tried to laugh it off, but I was mortified. I knew that this wasn't normal. But I also knew that I didn't really know what normal was.

I started reading again, but this time. I read about ADHD and Asperger's syndrome and high-functioning autism. I would show Wade lists of diagnostic criteria. "Look," I would say. "Just *look*!" He would look at the lists and then look at Henry and say, "He's fine. It's just a phase." When I would point to some of Henry's more quirky behaviors, including his obsessive interest in lawnmowers, which was still in full swing nearly two years after it began, Wade would say, "Lots of kids are odd. It doesn't mean that anything is wrong with him."

I also worried about how hyper Henry was. He hadn't walked until he was nearly 13 months old, but five days after taking his first unassisted steps, he was running from one end of our house to the other, at top speed. Henry would refuse to hold my hand and he would dart away in stores and airports and parking lots. I had lists of places

I couldn't take him because they were too difficult. I knew, I just *knew* that it wasn't supposed to be like this. I thought it was my fault, that he was eating too much sugar. I told my husband, "He can't have sugar. No more juice! No more cookies!" But when I would mention it to my parents or Wade's parents or my friends, this running and climbing and never being still, they would say, kindly and gently, "He's fine!'" or "Boys are like that!" or "Relax!" And I would think, my god, they're right, I'm a terrible mother. I started to wonder if I was overreacting. I just didn't know any more.

We spent two years looking for a preschool for Henry. We talked endlessly about what kind of school would be best and focus on his strengths. He was self-directed, we said. He would play by himself for hours. He was curious. He was smart. He could memorize entire books and recite them accurately. His vocabulary was huge and he spoke clearly and coherently. He was funny and kind. He liked to run and climb and play.

In the end, we chose a nice Montessori school. Henry went five mornings a week, for two and a half hours, and came home exhausted. He would nap for two or three hours, and still fall into bed at 7:30 and sleep all night. He never seemed to remember what he had done during the day; he would say, "I washed dishes." We assumed that he was just too tired and too young to really articulate what he was learning. We joked that he might have a career as a dishwasher in a fancy restaurant.

In February, we met with Henry's teacher for our regular conference. We had already decided that Henry wasn't ready for kindergarten, even though he would turn five over the summer. I wanted the teacher to know this before we met with her, so that she wouldn't worry that we might be upset or angry if she suggested it. When she called to schedule our conference, nearly a week before anyone else's, I told her that we felt that Henry would benefit from another year of preschool. After an odd silence, she agreed that this was a good idea. When we met with her, she nervously asked if we would be willing to have Henry evaluated by the school's psychologist. He was such a nice child, she said, kind and loving, but he was struggling in school, having a hard time doing what he was supposed to do. He was distracted and unfocused. He didn't really interact with the other children. He wasn't really learning anything.

Yes, we would like to have Henry evaluated. I was relieved that finally, someone else was seeing what I saw in Henry. Now, I thought, we will know what's going on. We will know what is wrong.

On Henry's fifth birthday, we sat on a yellow velvet sofa in the psychologist's office and listened as she talked through several months of observation and testing, and what seemed like hundreds of pages of questionnaires. Nothing she said was new to us; we were familiar with every behavior she described. We knew that Henry was hyper. We knew that he was distractible. We were beginning to know that he had trouble with social skills and with pragmatic language. What we had been missing, until that moment, was the external confirmation that something was not right. And now we had it.

The psychologist told us that Henry had ADHD and was at the high end of the scale for hyperactivity and distraction. She said that he had many of the characteristics of a child with Asperger's syndrome, but that she was not quite ready to diagnose him with that. Months later, in another doctor's office, this time with uncomfortable plastic chairs, Henry would be re-diagnosed with Non-Verbal Learning Disability and also Sensory Integration Dysfunction.

None of these labels tells me anything new about my son. None of them describes things I wasn't already seeing and worrying and reading about long before we had these names. None of them reveals anything I didn't already know about Henry. Instead, they reaffirmed that, all along, my son was different and that I was doing the best I could for him. In the psychologist's office, on Henry's fifth birthday, Wade looked at me and said, "You were right. You knew all along." I did. I just knew.

The Rhythm of Normal

Sheila Vakili

My son is twenty years-old now. At three, he was diagnosed with Neurofibromatosis, a genetic disorder. In layman's terms, the nerve endings in the brain are coated and can't transmit impulses normally. Most people know this condition by the common name of Elephant Man's Disease. It manifests itself in a variety of ways but Galen was "spared" the uncontrolled cell growth that deforms many of the afflicted. The major impact on him has been a seizure condition, delayed learning and emotional immaturity. I wish I could say that that's it, but the laundry list continues with scoliosis, a kidney that needed surgery to be repaired, removal of adenoids, tubes in the ears and probably some other things I've forgotten.

Early learning professionals told me that he probably wouldn't speak and wouldn't read. He tested so low I was basically told that he was retarded. They said I should accept it and do the best I could for him.

I wouldn't accept anything of the kind. I knew my son better than they did. I knew that he was capable of more and I refused to stick labels on him and try to make him fit into the neat little boxes educators and doctors had made up.

Nothing in life prepares you for this. You go through all the stages of grief. Your dreams for your child die but you still have a person to raise and a life to build. "Normal" and "average" have different meanings now.

You are slapped into an alternate universe where the roads are unfamiliar and the landscape is confusing and frightening. Each new emotion is overpowering and you are lost and alone on this new journey.

I recognize the path now. The steps are familiar to me; I have walked them many times in the last 17 years. I rage, cry, shake my fist at whatever god is listening, accept, forge forward, and start the cycle all over again. I decompress during the quiet times when his seizures are under control and hope that whatever comes next won't be too bad. I know that I will sleep but only after he is out of the hospital.

I feel guilty because I haven't done everything I could, read the right books, contacted the right doctor, pushed hard enough. I am failing him. I missed something. I feel inadequate and overwhelmed.

I struggle to give him his freedom, to let him grow up and away. I fight the fear of letting go, of letting him make his own mistakes. I depend on the goodness and understanding of strangers and pray that my faith is not misplaced.

I share Galen's joy when he accomplishes some simple pleasure and all is right in his world. I try not to be discouraged when his learning has stalled. I remind myself that there is always a plateau and then he jumps ahead.

I tune myself into the rhythms of his life. I know him better than I know any soul on this earth. I am not whole when he is gone.

I see the knowledge in his eyes; he is different. The sadness is sometimes more than my heart can hold. I try to love him enough to make the hurt go away. He is stronger than I think.

I'm glad that he can be stubborn and obnoxious because then I know that he will survive. I secretly cheer his transgressions because they prove he can be conniving and devious like any other kid.

I laugh at the absurdities of my life. How many mothers have their twenty year-old son booming out, "Can I sleep with you tonight?" while standing in line at the grocery store?

I decided long ago, that if there is a God, he gave me Galen so that I would never be alone and would always have someone who loved me.

I think I am right.

A Holland Tale

Paige Huskey

Once upon a time, not so long ago, a woman named Emily Perl Kingsley wrote a quaint story in which she attempts to describe what life is like when you have a child with a disability. She compares it to waiting, planning, and dreaming of a trip to Italy, but when you finally arrive, you find that your plane has landed in Holland instead. You have some adjustments to make, of course, but finally after things have settled, you're able to look around and see that Holland is not such a bad place after all. She concludes by writing that if you spent your whole life still wishing you'd gone to Italy, you'd be missing all of the wonderful things about Holland.

While I enjoyed the story, it didn't quite seem to account for our experience. You see, as it turns out, we were living in Holland for years, all the while believing we were in Italy. The Italian we had learned for our trip was of no use; the people in Italy spoke a language we'd never heard before. We tried to ask questions, we tried to communicate with the natives, but no one understood us. They sneered at us, gave us dirty looks. One thing was apparent; we weren't welcome in Italy.

While our son Shane had experienced problems since the early age of two and a half, no one ever doubted that they were things he would outgrow. We were told that his speech problems were typical, so we started speech therapy. Later, in preschool, his delayed fine motor skills caused no alarm, although the professionals working with him suggested that we hold him back from starting kindergarten. But he was so smart; we didn't feel that was the answer. When he did things like stare at the ceiling fan while making various faces and positioning his finger over one eye and then another, we thought it was cute even though it was during our evening meal every night. When he became preoccupied with freezing inanimate objects in water, we thought he was a budding scientist even though his fascination seemed to lie more in watching the objects melt than in collecting any data. The first time I found one of his plastics cups in the freezer, I was shocked. I could tell something was inside the now frozen water but couldn't actually make it out. When I asked Shane, who was four at the time and could just barely reach the freezer, what he'd done, he explained as best he could that he was interested in what would happen if he froze one of his toys. He sat the cup on the sink until the water had melted enough to release it from the cup and then he took out the cylindrical shaped ice and watched it melt in the sink. When he realized how long it was taking, he would go and play and come back every ten or fifteen minutes until the interior object was finally exposed and then examine it. He did this once or twice a week for several years, always trying out a new object or a different freezing method.

By age six, he was diagnosed with ADHD. He fit several of the criteria, and when we finally agreed to try medication, it did seem to help. Although very bright, he had difficulty staying on task and completing assignments at school and at home. We thought we were starting to understand and we tried desperately to fit in. Some people even attempted to help us. Despite the medication, the therapy, the school IEP, we still thought this was Italy. We were navigating the Italian maps now, but when we drove to the famous Florence, it wasn't there. We began to wonder what was wrong with us. We began to blame ourselves.

After his first couple of weeks in first grade at a new school, I decided to have lunch with him. I hadn't heard any concerns from the school so I assumed that he was doing well. While we walked in line, I noticed that Shane didn't seem too concerned with the little kids around him. I figured he was just shy and hadn't made any friends yet. After getting our food, we sat at the table with the rest of his class. Our tray lunch consisted of a corn dog, french fries, and red Jello. While Shane immediately started eating, I looked around realizing that we hadn't been given any eating utensils. I noticed the kids at the table passing a couple of baskets, so I assumed that was their purpose. When I looked back at Shane, however, he had already begun eating his Jello with his hands. I quietly asked him, "Shane, don't you know better than to eat with your hands?" He replied, "We have to, they don't give us any spoons."

I was heart broken. *How could he not notice the baskets on the table*, I wondered, *or ask someone for help?* So I asked another child at the table to pass a basket and explained to Shane that the eating utensils were to be found there, along with the napkins. He looked up for a second and simply replied, "Okay," then grabbed a spoon and continued with his Jello. Thinking about the previous two weeks, I realized that this explained why he had been coming home with such messy shirts every day. When I tried to talk to the teacher and then the school secretary about my concerns, they suggested that I was overreacting.

By age 11, our son was suicidal. His grades were falling, he couldn't keep friends, and most adults saw him as a trouble-maker. Shane's fifth grade teacher had decided that if Shane had not completed all of his homework for the day, he would stay in from recess to do so. After several weeks of this, Shane's anxiety and restlessness in the afternoons became uncontrollable. When we met with the teacher, we suggested that she phone or email us if Shane was missing an assignment and let us handle it in the evenings after Shane had had a break. We explained that his missing recess was likely the cause of much of his afternoon behavior. After much debate, she finally agreed, and this worked for awhile. But slowly over a period of several weeks, she began holding Shane in from recess again. We should have intervened immediately, but we didn't realize how fragile our son's emotional state had become. When we finally got a phone call from the school, we regretted our lax attitudes. The teacher had once again informed Shane that he would be missing recess due to some work that had not been completed. Shane, almost instantaneously, went into a meltdown and began biting his own forearms until he drew blood. When the teacher got help and they were able to calm Shane down enough to talk to him, he explained that he'd rather be dead than go on living another day under the current conditions.

We had reached the point where one doctor thought he might be on the verge of Bipolar Disorder, the school thought he was a behavior problem, and a therapist was determined that we were the cause of his disposition. Again, medication seemed to help, but we felt sure there was something still amiss. We were surrounded by people, yet we'd never been more lonely. We watched as others lived their lives, envying the way they seemed to know their place, they seemed to fit.

Now on a drug to treat depression, Shane's emotional state was much better, but his inability to fit in was becoming more and more apparent. At his sixth grade graduation, we were randomly assigned seats next to one of Shane's classmate's grandparents. When Shane found out which girl the grandparents belonged to, he became very interested and began asking them a multitude of questions. I was so proud that he was really attempting to engage these adults in conversation. Even while we tried to eat and listen to the program, however, he continued with more questions, begging them to tell him some funny stories about the girl when she was little. The grandparents looked befuddled, and I could tell their patience was running thin. So I finally leaned over and asked Shane why he was so preoccupied with hearing funny stories about this particular classmate. He responded, loud enough for the entire table to hear, that he wanted something to get her back with because of all the times she had teased and ridiculed him.

We recovered our composure the best we could and left immediately after dinner. We were thankful that we would not have to see these people again even though we dreaded Shane's transition to middle school.

We had prepared ourselves and him for the transition all summer, taking all of the precautionary measures we could think of, yet I sweated each day during the first couple of weeks, waiting for a phone call from the school. A few weeks into school, when I finally met with the school psychologist who was assigned to Shane, it was a day I'd never forget, a magical day. She asked me if I'd ever heard of Asperger's syndrome. When I told her I hadn't, she gave me some information to read and told me that she wanted to have some additional testing done on Shane. My husband was overseas, serving in Iraq at the time, but I'd never felt more reassured, more comforted.

When I read the material and did more research on my own, every-thing seemed to fit, everything started to make sense. I began to understand.

Our misguided journey was finally coming to an end. We began to pick up different guide books. We searched for doctors who could speak our language. Gradually, we began to see a change in the land-scape. Italy was beginning to look a lot like Holland. Of course the transition was difficult at first. After all, we still had to learn to speak their language and put their customs into practice. But ever so slow-ly, we began to fit in. And best of all, our son began to thrive in this new land where we'd always been, but were just beginning to realize and understand. We know now that Shane doesn't need "fixing," he just needs understanding and patience.

We thought our situation had been unique; after all we had been isolated and lonely before. Yet as we discovered Holland, we also discovered there were other families who'd been through exactly what we'd been through. You see, there are many people with Asperger's syndrome who are either misdiagnosed or undiagnosed. And for these people and their families who continue to believe they are in Italy, life can be miserable.

By the way, I've actually been to Italy. And while it is one of the most beautiful countries you'll ever see, with the most phenomenal, romantic, and picturesque structures and views, the reality is they have their own unique problems, too: the Italian Mafia, the rampant pollution, and let's not forget . . . Venice is sinking. Maybe we don't hear about their problems as often as we should or maybe they are downplayed so that we continue to desire that particular destination. But who decides our destination is any less grand, any less memorable? Sure Italy is a great place to visit, but I wouldn't want to live there.

Holland may sound like a faraway land full of enchantment and mystery, but if you take the time to look around and appreciate the world as it truly is, you'll find Holland is just down the street, at your local supermarket, or in your child's classroom.

Dream a Little Dream

Rhonda Pollero

Understandably, nearly everyone goes into parenting with similar dreams and expectations. Celebrating the first words, applauding the first steps, melting at that first smile. But for some of us, there comes a time when reality forces an adjustment in those dreams and expectations.

Unlike many parents, we knew going in that our daughter might have some cognitive and processing issues, the extent of which might not be evident until she started school. Did we have a prenatal test or a crystal ball? No. Our daughter was adopted from Russia, a country where Fetal Alcohol Syndrome and non-existent prenatal care are serious and often overlooked problems.

She was just over three when we brought her home and one of the first things we noticed was how fragile her teeth were and that she seemed to have some balance problems. Thanks to a great pediatric dentist, we learned that due to both a lack of appropriate prenatal nutrition and the result of alcohol abuse on the part of her birth mother, she had no enamel on her teeth. Now, this may seem like a minor, cosmetic inconvenience, but there is more to it. As her teeth began to break off at the gum line, she became a target of her peers. This, coupled with her speech issues. made those early days difficult for her to fit in. Kids can be cruel, especially when they can't or don't understand the problem. My daughter's teeth weren't discolored and black because of poor hygiene but from genetics and circumstance.

In the last six years, we have been able to correct many of her dental problems, though she's had veneers and braces on her teeth since the age of four and there's really no end in sight. The braces, while correcting her teeth, exacerbated her speech difficulties. They worsened her speech impediment. After some time with a speech therapist, this situation is slowly resolving itself.

As it turns out, she didn't have balance issues, she had a serious vision defect. Because of the Fetal Alcohol Syndrome, the muscles in her eyes were negatively impacted by the in-vitro alcohol abuse. She was fitted for thick glasses and is required to patch her weaker eye for most of the day. Again, this subjected her to ridicule at the hands of her peers. Her vision is correctable to 20/100. That means she will not be eligible to drive when the time comes, though there are experimental surgeries on the horizon, so perhaps in five years, there will be a potential treatment that will allow her to reach that milestone.

By far, the biggest challenge we face are her information processing issues. Luckily, she has a relatively mild form of the syndrome, but that seems to have worked against us rather than in our favor. She doesn't test low enough to qualify for special education, but she isn't able to work at grade level without a great deal of tutoring for reinforcement. Thirty minutes of homework for an average child takes her about two hours to complete and by the next morning, she's incapable of recalling roughly 75% of the covered material.

The worst part of all this is the guilt. Not hers, mine. It breaks my heart when she comes home after a particularly rough day at school.

Children reared in orphanages, even if only for three years, crave peer acceptance. They have a part-of-the-group mentality and a high need to be included. My daughter is often excluded and/or ignored because she is 'different.'

It has been very hard to reconcile my expectations of what her life would be like with us and the reality of what it is. I find myself resentful of parents who fail to teach their children not to tease, bully and/or taunt. I've learned that maybe one of the greatest gifts you can give any child is an understanding of the importance of compassion. It's very hard to accept that unconditional, parental love alone won't be enough to ease pain or protect them from the world.

I'm still amazed that after providing her school with documentation regarding her history, they required me to have her tested for ADD and ADHD. If your child doesn't concentrate, the default position seems to be label them and drug them. ADD and ADHD are not the only reasons a child has difficulty processing information and/or is easily distracted in a classroom setting. Granted, my daughter is an exception, but with a growing number of foreign adoptions, it would help if school systems would at least attempt to educate themselves on the effects of Fetal Alcohol Syndrome.

Ironically, I find myself less angry at her irresponsible birth mother. At least she made the decision to allow her child to be adopted. I firmly believe that regardless of my daughter's challenges, we are much better equipped to make sure she can get all the help she might need than if she'd languished in a Russian orphanage.

My daughter has taught me the real meaning of excellence. For more than forty years, I thought the Holy Grail of education was doing

'A' work. Nothing could be farther than the truth. Excellence is celebrating the uniqueness and individuality of your child's accomplishes. Forget the 'A,' congratulate the 'C' and reward the 'B.' File those 'Fs" away with a positive reminder that next week he or she gets a fresh start and they can succeed.

Be ready to do battle. Battle doesn't have to mean confrontation. Communicate with the teachers, specialists or whoever is in a position to get you what you need or send you where you need to go to get your child what he or she needs. Find resources that might help your child. Pay for it out of your own pocket if necessary–you're investing in your child's future. Don't accept 'we can't' or 'we won't.'

Don't try to go it alone. In a perfect world, your spouse/child's father will take an active role. For whatever reason, many men often take longer to recognize and confront problems. And for a lot of reasons, women seem to be more proactive in researching and seeking out alternatives and/or specialists to cope with the disabilities and challenges their children face. But a child with special needs is a family problem–everyone is affected–requiring family intervention and support. If that isn't a possibility, find a friend. Someone you can share the tragedies and triumphs with as you navigate the day in and day out reality of parenting your child. Try support groups. Try anything and everything that allows you better cope. You'll be better able to handle things if you don't feel isolated, alone, frustrated.

Call the critics. I can't tell you how often I hear "well, if she'd just apply herself," or "she'd do better in school if you punished her for failure." At the risk of sounding cliché, until they've walked a day in your shoes, they don't get an opinion. My situation is compounded by the fact that our son passed away at the age of 13 waiting for a heart transplant, so I also get, "You spoil her because you lost Kyle. You don't demand enough of her." Yes, the death of my son made me a different person, but that has nothing to do with my daughter's Fetal Alcohol Syndrome.

Give yourself permission to grieve. Wanting to be a 'normal' family is a reasonable and understandable desire. Some days are so hard you simply want to cry. You need to cry. So cry. Do it unapologetically but privately, particularly if your child can comprehend the ideas of sadness and frustration.

But at the end of the day, when I tiptoe into her room and watch her sleep, I don't see a child with fetal alcohol syndrome or visual impairment or a speech impediment or even hear the ca-ching of the years of dental work ahead. I see the beautiful nine year-old who saved me from the despair of losing my son. I see a little girl who can do or be anything she wants within the confines of her disabilities. Above all, I see a child who, in spite of the daily taunts and cruel remarks of her peers, knows she is unconditionally loved.

Dancing with Despair

Caryn Sullivan

I can't pinpoint the person who first spoke the word "autism." I do recall with great certainty that I could not repeat the word for months after I first heard it. I didn't really know what it meant; I just knew that it was not good.

I now know that it is something bigger than I could ever have imagined; that it wrought changes in my life that I would never have anticipated, pushing me to limits I didn't know I had. I now know that it is an extremely isolating disorder and that it is a black hole that seems endless.

I was four months pregnant with our daughter when I tearfully told my law colleagues about Jack's diagnosis of autism. I informed them I would be taking a leave of absence to "take care of it." Little did I know how my life was about to change. Little did I know how lonely the subsequent years would be.

In the early phase, post-diagnosis, I moved about in a state of shocked disbelief, searching for the captain of the ship that would take him to the land of normalcy. I was looking for someone to hand me a road map and a game plan so that we could take care of this problem. I am, after all, the consummate problem solver. After awhile, I began to realize that there was no captain waiting to be found. The game plan was unwritten. There were foot soldiers and there were plays. But, there was only one person who was going to put it all together. That was me. Thus, 13 years later, I remain an unemployed advocate for my son and the captain of the ship.

Although my husband is very supportive now, his support has ebbed and flowed. Ted has a full-time law practice and three other children, and has only so much time and energy to devote to the cause. In the early years, the angry years, he told me that Jack would have to be institutionalized. I made it clear that would never happen and he never broached the topic again.

Typically, his strength has been as the relief pitcher. When Jack was younger, Ted would frequently drop everything and come home during the bewitching hour when I could no longer handle the stress of the child who never stopped moving. But when it came to doing the mind-numbing research, he drew the line. He ignored the stack of autism reading materials that I placed on his night stand. While I read about autism, he read about business, politics, law and sports. If I wanted to pursue more traditional approaches to autism, he typically concurred. But as my research expanded and I learned more about "cutting edge" approaches and practitioners, he became more skeptical and unsupportive. Typically, I ignored his uninformed opinions and moved forward without him. I resented the lack of support but was undeterred in my mission. I was going to solve the mystery, with or without him. Recently, however, he has changed his views and is actively getting in the game. Often employing humor, he serves as a wonderful role model for the son who so desperately needs one. At last, a first mate.

From the beginning, I have struggled to ascertain what we should reasonably expect from Jack. The professionals made it clear they could not predict what the future would hold for him. For a person who likes things to be concrete, watching my life unfold as if projected on an antenna-free television screen has been extraordinarily frustrating. I see things in black and white; the fuzzy picture is excruciating for me. Tell me what I'm dealing with and I will accept it. Keep me in the dark and I will try to manage the stress by becoming a control freak.

The conventional wisdom when Jack was diagnosed was that the brain was elastic so we needed to seize the window of opportunity and employ the early intervention strategies while the brain was still elastic. Ah, a plan. I threw myself into the job of trying to "fix him" before time ran out. If I just took him to speech therapy, if I just took him to occupational therapy, if we just tried this drug, if we just got him into swimming, if we just gave him these nutritional supplements, we could make it all better so that we could get our lives back, live our dreams, save our marriage, and give our family the kind of life we'd envisioned. Time and money were irrelevant. All that mattered was the goal.

Hence, the dance with despair: the raging battle between hopefulness and hopelessness that consumes me. In my search for "a cure," I have taken Jack to more than 40 health professionals for one issue or another, for not only does he have developmental delays, he also has chronic, complicated and confusing medical issues. We have seen neurologists, psychologists, psychiatrists, pediatricians, gastroenterologists, urologists, cardiologists, orthopedists, speech therapists, occupational therapists, vision therapists, and more. I have filled out dozens of medical forms, each time reliving the heartache as I recounted his development and regression, his symptoms, and related the treatments we've tried, embraced and discarded. I've had to bite my tongue to keep from screaming, "Can't someone develop a universal medical history form?" I've traveled across the country to attend autism conferences. I've spent countless hours on the Internet. Several years ago, hoping to eliminate embarrassing vomiting and soiling problems, I put the whole family on a restricted diet, much to their dismay. To understand what I was doing, I spent hours in grocery store aisles reading food labels, learning about gluten, casein, dyes, phenols, and more. I learned that, among other things, the omnipresent corn syrup is like poison to Jack and must be avoided at all costs to prevent extremely embarrassing episodes of public vomiting. I literally went the extra mile by driving to a specialty grocery store in an effort to acquire expensive and often tasteless food for my family. To my delight, and my dismay, I found that the diet helped. Among other things, the vomiting dissipated. *Hope.* But, the diet is expensive and burdensome to execute faithfully and my family did not like gluten free food! I have minimal time to cook and spending extra time in the kitchen was not on my top ten list of favorite activities. *Despair.*

Although we had accumulated a huge supply of Happy Meal toys in the early years, I eventually decided that I was going to break our fast food habit. One day, however, I capitulated and took Jack to McDonald's. As we drove up to the drive-through window, he looked up at the big sign with the yellow arches and said, "Look mom. Billions and billions served. What do you have to say about that, health food Nazi?" Ah, that marvelous sense of humor!

Some days, I feel that I have much to celebrate; other days I feel I have much to mourn. Clearly, Jack has made great progress. I know there are parents of autistic kids who would do anything to have a child who functions as well as him. Knowing that doesn't make it any easier to live with him, doesn't make me feel less stressed, and doesn't make me feel less concerned for the future. For years, we lived on a roller coaster ride that was driven by his moods, his activity level, his toileting travesties, and his chronic sleeplessness. We never knew from day to day what we would be dealing with. If he was calm, the household was calm. If he was revved up, the stress level in the household increased commensurately. I only relaxed completely when he was asleep.

Whether it is the result of all of the medicine, supplements, diet, therapy, or just plain old maturing, we will never know for sure, but he is more stable and high functioning now than he has ever been. I have this image of him, suspended in mid-air between the severely challenged and the very capable. His skills are very scattered and his motivation is elusive. If we are going on vacation, he is the first up and dressed, without a word from us. *Hope.* On school days, however, we either hound him to get moving or let him lie there and earn yet another tardy. *Despair.* The non-verbal, hyperactive toddler who we called "Jumping Jack Flash" has become a sedentary, electronically-addicted teenager who rarely moves any body part other than his fingers. The good news is he has a heart of gold. I can stumble out of bed in the morning, hair pointing in all directions, and he will tell me how beautiful I am. *Hope.*

Although we re-board the roller coaster at times, our rides are less frequent and the cars on the coaster don't make as many quick, jerking stops as they once did. But the ride goes on and the stress, my constant companion, remains.

But…he talks. He makes up his own jokes. He reads voraciously. With a written list in hand, Jack can perform increasingly more tasks well. He is learning to do household chores. He is taking responsibility for his personal hygiene. He is taking his medication on his own. He has been much more helpful to me lately and much less resistant to contributing to the household. At times, life feels almost normal. *Hope.*

Lately, he seems to be growing up so quickly. Some days I wonder where the time has gone. Even our older kids cannot believe Jack is now a high school sophomore. I flash back on the first day of kindergarten and the image of neighbor kids climbing aboard the big yellow school bus. With a knot in my stomach, I recall the memory of the small yellow bus driving off with my son belted in. *Despair.*

They are all teenagers now. My friends are taking their teens to driver's education classes. I'm taking my teen to speech therapy, behavioral therapy, social skills group, and gastroenterology workups. Some days I can hardly bear to hear these friends talk about their kids. They are going to homecoming; they are having sleepovers; they are going to sports camps. Each time I hear about something that those kids are doing, *things my kid should be doing,* I die another death. While I don't consider myself a petty person, at times I am consumed by envy. Their kids have a posse of friends to spend their days, nights, weekends, and vacations with. They ride the big yellow bus to school.

My friends have family members or neighbors who will take their kids so that they can take a trip with their husbands. Our families are not in a position to help us. The best they can do is listen and offer long distance emotional support and say they wish they lived closer so they could help us. How I wish that were so! Virtually every person who has ever helped us with Jack has been on our payroll.

While we've had offers to help, the need is so great that we've still come up short. I know there are those who want to help but are hesitant to do so. And who can blame them? I would probably be no different. He sucks the energy right out of you through his stubborn resistance to almost every new idea, activity, place or food. While at times he behaves appropriately, there is always that lingering uncertainty about what he might do or say next. There's always that gnawing fear that it all might fall apart at any moment.

Surely, some days, my friends and family can barely stand to hear me talk about my kid. The litany of concerns is endless. He hasn't slept through the night for two weeks; he throws up when he goes to a new camp; he has back pain; he plays video games and computer games for hours on end; he has no friends. I can hear it in their voices when they feel that they have exhausted their supply of ideas or they are frustrated that I haven't taken other suggestions, and they have nothing else to offer. I understand when they suggest that I join a support group and take my worries and complaints to a venue where people may actually know what to say. They don't understand how terrifying it can be to hear another parent in a support group relate an experience that renders you hopeless. Hope must be hoarded at all costs.

I have burdened my friends and family with my fears, frustrations, and challenges and will always be grateful that they have not abandoned me. I realize, though, that when they are looking for someone to have a good laugh with, I'm not on the short list to call. As life has marched on, my friends have joined tennis leagues and golf leagues, and gone away on girls' weekends. Occasionally, I have been invited to participate, but I rarely feel that I can fit in the fun. I spend my time at medical offices or autism workshops or searching for a new social worker while managing his dozen plus daily medications and supplements. I've cast aside the dreams I once had for a different, more normal, life. I've found it easier to deny the dreams than to acknowledge the loss because I fear that once I let in the pain it will consume me and I won't be able to do what I need to do.

My husband has been a bit more honest and vocal about the loss of the life he had envisioned. In the depths of my mind, I know that Ted has taken the back seat to our son's needs. I rationalize that he is able to walk, talk, use the bathroom, dress himself, and go out in public without my help. And, he has had more freedom to live his dreams, although he has shouldered the unexpected burden of being the sole breadwinner. In my view, he has the luxury of taking many "guy trips" because he only needs to clear his work calendar. It is exhausting for me to prepare to go away and emotionally draining to return to my reality so my getaways are more infrequent.

It is equally difficult to balance my younger daughter's needs. Her frustration has grown over the years and often surfaces in her silent but obvious disapproval of my parenting. I sense her judgment. Her gaze says, you need to punish him for that; he shouldn't get away with that. It's not fair. Trying to balance the equities among siblings is no easy task. Why must she, the younger sibling, assume responsibilities that have not been placed on him as well? Why does he get a pass for behaviors that would never be acceptable from her? I know intuitively that she has become the perfect child because he is not. My work is cut out for me and she perceives that there is no room for another challenging child within our domain.

The older children, who lived with us part time, sacrificed precious time with their dad, despite our efforts to balance everyone's needs. Fortunately, Caitie and Dan have been loving and patient, although

they experienced many silent moments of frustration and embarrassment – the inevitable result of having a sibling with an invisible
disability who can't or won't do many things they enjoy. Thankfully,
when they lived at home, they often provided me with the few
moments of respite I needed to make it through the day. To their
credit, Caitie and Dan have never complained (to me) or expressed
the resentment that one could expect. Dan has come home from
college more than once to help out in a crisis. I often wish he lived
closer so he could teach Jack all the guy stuff that he has not learned
from his peers.

In an effort to expose him to other kids and give him something to
do outside our home, I enrolled Jack in a social skills group, thinking that perhaps he could make just one new friend, someone to hang
out with during the torturously long summer. *Hope.* Alas, the
program ended and he has not one new friend, but two new enemies.
His assessment of the program: it was "more boring than church," an
opinion I shared after reviewing the curriculum. *Despair.*

In spite of all the struggles, life with Jack has not just been about
giving to him. He has given back in spades. The boy who has always
been intrigued by superheroes recently became our family's super-
hero. At the age of 10, our bright, athletic, social butterfly of a
daughter was diagnosed with a rare blood disorder. Her only hope
was a bone marrow transplant. To have the transplant, she needed a
donor. Without hesitation, Jack, who loathes needles, had his blood
drawn to determine if he was a match. Afterwards, he looked at his
sister from the corner of his eye and said, "So Julia, did they give you
my mojo yet?" By a great stroke of luck, and against the odds, Jack
was her perfectly matched donor. He subsequently gave her his magic
"mojo." Just before the transplant, his teacher sent home a poem he

wrote called "The Operation."

I am giving bone marrow to my Sis.
I'm going to the hospital Tuesday.
When I'm done she will have a good life kiss.
Julia gets my marrow soon, Hooray!
I will be staying overnight, one night.
In the hospital they have beds of fluff.
The operation fills me with some fright
Because of this we will get lots of stuff.
In the hospital I will read a book.
I will get some medicine by I.V.
Some people will be kind to us and cook.
Julia will be better, yes siree!
The transplant is the coolest thing I've known.
Julia will get better and come home!

Julia did get better and she did come home. It is ironic that Jack, the needy one, saved Julia, the child who seemingly needed so little. It was a totally selfless, priceless act from the one person in our family who can suck all of the oxygen out of the room. As a mother who loves them both with all my heart, I can barely comprehend the enormity of it all. Did he realize the importance of his gift? It's hard to know.

I do know that there was a cost to him, though. Julia's illness presented me with a legitimate reprieve from "fixing" Jack. In a truly bizarre way, the three weeks I spent at the hospital with Julia while she received a life-threatening treatment for a life-threatening illness felt like a vacation. There were few expectations of me during that time period, other than to care for Julia alongside a world-renowned transplant team. I had arranged for other people to manage Jack's needs. For the first time in her life, I felt like I could give Julia my complete attention. In a perverse way, this exceedingly rare, life-threatening illness gave me a much needed opportunity to bond with my daughter. We spent so many hours together that it was almost as if we became one. She paid a huge price for us to have this time together but I'm certain that it never would have happened otherwise.

During Julia's exhausting and extended recovery period, Jack's needs were basically an afterthought for me and an add-on for my extremely busy husband. Jack passed the time by watching television for hours each day. The characters were his companions and the television was his babysitter. A year passed without my vigilant focus on his needs. During that year, he started high school and made a new friend. Grant has been a godsend. When they are together, Jack acts like a typical teenager, playing video games and complaining about unpopular teachers. He told me that he likes having Grant for a friend because they are so much alike. He, like all of us, wants to be understood – *Hope.*

Now that Julia has resumed her life without weekly doctor visits and blood draws, my attention has shifted back to Jack, with a new urgency. Critical time was lost during which I was not working to "fix him." He has three years left in high school. The window is almost closed. My instincts tell me there is still so much left to be done before he is "fixed" – *Despair.* But my heart tells me I must slow down. The truth is, I am worn out. An enormous amount of stress has insinuated itself into my life through terrifying illnesses. In a span of 10 years, our family has powered through Ted's heart attack, my breast cancer, and Julia's bone marrow transplant while dealing with the daily challenges of autism. Having gone all these years without the crew I needed, this captain feels depleted, discouraged and daunted by the decisions and work that lie ahead.

With newfound clarity, I realize it is time to sail this ship out of the fog and into the harbor.

My heart now lighter, I have a new game plan. I am not going to fix Jack. I am going to enjoy life with my husband, our daughters, *both* sons, friends and other family members. I am going to take trips, write stories, ski, bike, walk, laugh, and cry. I will also help Jack to prepare for an independent life. When the time comes, I will help him to find a suitable home of his own and help him to pursue his own educational or employment goals. While he will never be a lawyer, he could happily work in a library or a bookstore. Perhaps some day he might find the woman of his dreams. Like the professionals, I do not have a crystal ball. However, it is becoming quite clear to me that Jack must become the captain of his own ship. I'm beginning to believe that he can do it. I'm beginning to believe that he might actually like being "Captain Jack!"

Doing What I Could Do

Janice Noble

I could write the words that would be pleasant, easier to hear. I could write about the incredible, destructible behaviors my special needs child exhibits. I could write something inspirational, about the lessons I have learned. I could be angry and bitter and keep asking why God did this to me. I could use my daughter's disability to give me automatic enrollment into a group that stands for a good cause. I could lecture you about the disease itself, or I could just write the words that come as I sit here today.

Where do I begin? Where is my starting point? Life begins, a chronological order of events follow, and there is an ending. I do not, of course, know how my story will end. The greatest celebration is that I do not care. It is not because I have given up, nor is it because I feel that I need to do something impressionable, of importance, to be of inspiration. It is now so perfectly clear. But for years, it wasn't clear at all.

Most of us who have been slammed with the devastating news that our child is developmentally disabled react similarly. The usual fog sets in, followed by denial, sadness and anger. We move on to disappointment and fine tune our grief and bitterness, while at the same time we acknowledge our loss of normalcy. We give up on dreams, reset the barometer, step up as our child's advocate, and adjust to a life within our limitations. But it does not always get better for everyone.

I spent years doing all the right things. I spent time with parents, who like me, were raising a special needs child. I encouraged my child to enjoy those things that only normal children do, I expended energy into "showing her the world" and overlooked the many flaws that would never allow her to reach what I wanted her to be capable of. I shared my story in the newspaper, hoping it might help others. I received the compliments that I grew to hate. "God knew you were special enough to give a special child to." How I despised that one in particular

I was great at ignoring the judgmental stares as my child pulled things off the shelves at the grocery store. I did a lot of things right. I cared. I never stopped caring.

I knew everything and at the same time, I knew nothing. I had no answers as her disabilities became more apparent. I was constantly reminded of her limitations and I cried oceans of tears. I lost interest in simple things. I was gut- wrenched with sadness, failure and dis-appointment, desperate to feel something other than sadness. I sought out quick fixes to other emotions, a variety of self-destructive behaviors that I will leave to your imagination.

But the sun always came up each day. I had other children, a husband, family and friends that needed me. This put more pressure on me to find that peaceful place and start living instead of merely existing.

I could tell you that my life became a struggle, with details too boring for others to listen to. My marriage was over and a divorce was inevitable. I hated knowing that I was the one who needed to be strong, who needed to make decisions. I could tell you that some great light shone upon me and a great idea revealed itself.

Or, I could continue to be truthful and let you know that my circumstances changed, for the worst, both financially and emotionally. I could bore you with facts that even I do not look at anymore. I will tell you I waited, I hoped and I prayed for the situation to change.

The fact of the matter is nothing has changed. The challenges grow. My daughter's disability is here, now and forever and no wishing it away, nor wanting it to be different even matters. I can tell you that this is my journey, it is mine. It has been long, it has been difficult and my story is yet to be over.

I can tell you that God has blessed me with insight. Insight that came with a price that has been paid. It has come freely, it has come abundantly, and it has come with hope.

It has come with acceptance and with choice. Acceptance comes more easily to some than to others. But that, in the end, is not of importance. We are equipped to accept and I have.

My daughter has awakened the core of who I was meant to be, who I have become, and who I will always be. She has been my teacher, my strength, my hope. She is the one who has empowered me. My daughter is flawless, impressionable, innocent, and all that is pure. She is life. She is contagious. She is simple in the complexity of this world. She is my blessing. Her special needs were the catalyst for me to change into the person I needed to be. In the end, you see, it was me that was disabled. Today I choose to accept, hope, love and be all that I can be for myself and my daughter. I now know that we are both perfect exactly the way we are.

The Red Herring

Michele Ackerman

Each time I see the scar across the top of my daughter's head I am reminded of what I'm most grateful for. To me, her ear to ear scar symbolizes all of the lessons I painfully learned during the summer of 2004.

Our beautiful daughter was born with a tiny cleft lip, a mucosal tag, wide set eyes and a sacral dimple. At birth, our doctors reassured us that her cleft lip and mucosal tag on her lip was nothing to worry about but the dimple in her spine needed to be evaluated. At four weeks old she had an MRI of her lower spine which ruled out Spina Bifida. At four months old, she had her cleft lip repaired. I noticed, at about six months-old, that one of her eyes wandered. At about the same time we noticed she had a strange faint line down the middle of her nose. No one could explain that. She was, however, developing normally and met her milestones on time. The geneticist told us to enjoy our gorgeous little girl and not to worry.

At age three she had eye surgery to correct her weak eye muscles. She suffered from recurrent ear infections and from six months on, every morning for a few hours had a chronic clear drainage out of her nose. She had two more surgeries to place, and then replace ear tubes. During the later part of her fourth year, she began to complain that her feet frequently fell asleep. After several months, a trip to an ortho-

pedist, and weekly physical therapy sessions, her feet continued to
fall asleep with increased frequency. My mother's instinct began to
yell loudly that something was just "not right". A discussion with our
pediatrician led to a referral to a pediatric neurosurgeon. The neurosurgeon examined her then ordered a spine and a brain MRI.

My heart felt heavy as we drove to the consult meeting to discuss the
MRI results. I will never forget the day that my husband and I stared
at the images of our daughter's brain on the computer screen as the
neurosurgeon spoke to us. She took a deep breath and then gently
explained that very early in our daughter's fetal development her
skull did not fully close. As a result, part of her brain had actually
slipped through this gap and was now outside of her skull, but still
inside her head. The scan seemed to indicate that this part of her
brain was dragged down behind the bridge of her nose and was
extending as far down as the roof of her mouth. There was more. The
doctor then compassionately described the rarity of this condition, a
basal encephalocele, which she told us is almost never initially diagnosed in 5 year-olds. She handed me a tissue as I began to quietly cry.
Then the news got even worse. Our daughter's pituitary gland, hypo-
thalamus, optic chiasm and optic nerves were all "involved" in this
defect. The doctor pinpointed on the MRI images exactly how our
daughter's optic nerves and other brain tissue had been adjusted and
re-routed. The MRI also revealed dysgenesis of the corpus callosum a
rare congenital abnormality of the structure of her brain. In complete
shock, we stared at the picture of our youngest child's brain on the
computer screen trying to comprehend the enormity of it all.

Remarkably, our daughter, unbeknownst to all of us, walked around
for five years with these secret defects lurking inside her head. It was
unbelievable. The whole scenario seemed like a motion picture with
my daughter in the starring role.

Due to the rarity of her diagnosis, her doctors told us they needed a lot more information about what was exactly going on "in there." The carefree summer that I had planned quickly evolved into one filled with too many trips to the hospital, too many brain MRI's and CT scans, way too much anesthesia, and not enough trips to the pool. The cliché about the best laid plans rang true.

At first I spent the days wearing a perfect poker face, trying to keep myself together for my children but when they went to bed, I went into the bathroom and sobbed. I sat on the cold bathroom floor and let the painful tears flow. I mourned the loss of an ordinary childhood for my sweet little girl, I cried for her future and what she was about to endure. I cried because I felt sorry for myself and my family. Then, while waiting for a surgery date, the anger crept in. I just didn't know who to direct it towards. I didn't drink any alcohol or caffeine while pregnant. There was no family history of even a cleft lip. My pregnancy was uneventful and included all the recommended pre-natal testing.

After she was born and throughout her first five years of life our daughter was seen by countless doctors at reputable children's hospitals and not one of them caught it. Her condition was just so rare, almost unthinkable, really. Even the neurosurgeon who diagnosed it was shocked by what she saw on the MRI. My anger was short-lived. I realized that it wouldn't serve anyone, most of all my daughter who so desperately needed me. I began to accept the fact that this was my daughter's life, her path and I was here to help her through it. So, I decided to focus my energies on getting her the treatment she needed and keeping our family intact through this ordeal. I mustered up strength from deep in my soul and I got up off the bathroom floor. I had to prepare myself and my family for the challenges of whatever the future had in store.

Just when I thought it couldn't get any worse, another more invasive scan revealed that our daughter's brain had "sprung a leak" For as far back as I could recall, our daughter had a runny nose for a few hours every morning. It puzzled me for years. Her pediatrician at the time explained the chronic morning drip as either allergies or back to back colds. Needless to say, the CT scan that summer told a very different story. The fluid that was leaking out of her nose every morning was cerebral spinal fluid (CSF) and it was coming from her brain. In fact, it was not a cold or allergies. I seemed to be the only one not surprised by this news. I finally had the answer to her chronic morning runny nose.

The danger, our doctors explained, in having spinal fluid dripping out of her nose through a hole in her brain meant that bacteria could travel up her nose and via the hole have direct access to her brain. In other words, it meant a huge meningitis risk. The doctors shook their heads in wonderment as we all discussed the fact that she had never contracted bacterial meningitis. Then, in no uncertain terms, her doctors made it perfectly clear that it was time to stop tempting fate. All second, third and fourth opinions agreed. Brain surgery was her only option. It was not going to be an easy surgery.

Until then, I never thought much about the sense of smell. I took it for granted until I learned that our daughter might lose her sense of smell forever, as a result of the brain surgery she was about to undergo.

They broke the news to us at one of the many pre-surgical planning meetings we attended. Our daughter's neurosurgeon rattled off the long list of the risks associated with her upcoming brain surgery. She started with the generic ones, and then proceeded to tell us another more serious list of possible outcomes unique to our daughter's rare situation. This other list began with a host of visual disturbances or blindness; a 50/50 chance of pituitary gland damage; various neurological damage; and finally, an almost 100% certainty of a permanent loss of her sense of smell. We knew there were risks, but this information was almost too much to digest. Other than a few sighs, the car ride home that day was dreadfully quiet.

I was haunted daily by the possible outcomes from brain surgery. I had nightmares of my daughter screaming "mommy, I can't see anything" and feared that she would have a host of pituitary problems requiring constant monitoring and daily medications. I envisioned our family spending months at the children's hospital, her having no memory or other neurological problems, and of course, every other horrible possible combination of it all. But worst of all, I feared her death. The thought of her living without her sense of smell never even entered my thoughts. I classified the possible loss of smell as "no big deal" It surprised me to discover that no one else agreed.

My husband was quite disturbed by the prospect and was appalled when I announced that I could care less about her ever smelling again. Then later over lunch my dearest friends, in unison, agreed with my husband's viewpoint. To me it all sounded a bit absurd. How could anyone think about the practically useless sense of smell while all the other possible horrific surgical outcomes hung over our heads? Then one day while at the beach breathing in all my favorite smells I began to actually consider what her life would be like without the sense of smell.

So, I conducted my own research. I learned that humans use smell to continuously sample the environment for information. Some scientists suggest that smell can influence mood, memory, emotions, mate choice, the immune system and human hormones. A quick read through an old college physiology book helped explain how the sense of smell works in our bodies.

I attended the next surgical meeting armed with this information and asked how it applied to our daughter's potential loss of smell. The doctor patiently explained that after our daughter's skull was opened she would have to very carefully maneuver her way through olfactory nerves and receptors. It was the most direct route. Her goal was to not sever any of the olfactory nerves in the process. She also mentioned that surgically it would be faster to cut right through those nerves as some colleagues had suggested. After the explanation, she shared a joke about the olfactory nerves that is often told within the neurosurgeon community. The punch line went something like this, "The olfactory nerves are so sensitive that sometimes all you have to do is look at them the wrong way and the sense of smell is wiped out." While I especially appreciated the joke and her willingness to share it I didn't hold out much hope that my daughter would ever smell again. This time, however, it bothered me.

Many days, it was my sense of humor that saved me. Throughout the latter part of this whole ordeal, I possessed the uncanny ability to find and appreciate humor wherever and whenever I could. In fact, when it came to the sense of smell good joke material was easy to find. One day at yet another pre-surgical meeting my mind began to wander, just a little. As I was studying our neurosurgeon's pregnant belly, I began to daydream about myself pregnant. I was suddenly bombarded by vivid memories of me cursing my own sense of smell. It became my arch enemy. I remembered being completely repulsed by the scent of certain spices and having to spend an entire Thanksgiving dinner in the bathroom. My mind then raced to the future arriving at the day of my daughter's surgery. I envisioned our pregnant neurosur-

geon opening up our daughter's skull. I chuckled, quietly, as I imagined her getting sick to her stomach from the vile smells that would
most certainly accompany brain surgery. I shared my daydream with
two of my closest friends and we giggled at the prospect of our super-
hero neurosurgeon needing a barf bag in the middle of my daughter's
very delicate brain surgery. I didn't share my jokes with everyone.
Some people could not understand how I could laugh "at a time like
this." Despite their criticisms, I found the humor and laughed when
I could. It felt good.

Finally, five months after her diagnosis, in what seemed like an
eternity, our daughter's operation day arrived. After 13 long hours of
meticulous brain surgery the neurosurgeon emerged.

She gave us the news we waited months to hear. Our daughter had
survived the surgery and was in ICU on a ventilator. She lost one pint
of blood, but did well overall. Once inside her head, they discovered
the encephalocele was bigger then they had anticipated. They were
surprised to find that brain tissue had also protruded into her nasal
cavity like a sail. We could see the exhaustion in the doctor's face as
she continued with her report. She explained how she gently lifted
the brain tissue off of the roof of her mouth and out of her nose. She
described the reinforcement bone they built to protect her brain that
would still, forever remain outside of her skull but inside her head.
She smiled as she spoke of how she wished that she could have just
pushed her brain back into her skull, where it belonged and closed it
off for good. However, she resisted the urge because of the damage it
would have caused to her functioning brain. There was a lot to report
but we hung on her every word. She explained how she sealed the
spinal fluid leak with some special glue.

Then last, she told how she delicately maneuvered through the sea of olfactory nerves without having to cut any of them. Her technique, she explained, added over two hours to the operation. Nevertheless, it was still a certainty that our daughter's sense of smell would be diminished immediately after the surgery. She reminded us to hold out hope because she did everything in her power in an attempt to save it. Only time would tell. Later, as I replayed her post surgical report in my head, for the tenth time, it occurred to me that maybe, just maybe, the sense of smell was worth saving after all.

The next three days in the intensive care unit were filled with worry and fear as we waited for our daughter's body to wake up. She was on a ventilator, her face was completely swollen and her eyes were only slits. She had IV lines in every limb, a catheter, a bandage on her head, a central IV line and an arterial IV line in her neck. I prepared myself for how she would look after surgery, but it was still horrifying. Gradually the good news began to roll in. Her pupils were dilating, and she appeared neurologically intact. Her pituitary gland function was somewhat questionable but seemed within normal limits in her post operative state. Each day brought better reports and bigger smiles from her doctors. Then she managed to shock us all yet again with her speedy recovery. Just short of two weeks later, in what was the ultimate gift to me, our five year- old daughter left the hospital intact, but without her sense of smell. I however, felt like I had been hit by a truck.

At home, she recovered even faster. But she still couldn't smell a thing. Initially she complained that food tasted funny and had no real appetite but she soon adjusted. After only a few weeks it seemed that she didn't care that much about her inability to smell. I, on the other hand, became obsessed with it. Every few days, I would shove some pungent item under her nose and ask her if she could smell it. For months, her reply was always the same, "No, mommy, I can't smell it."

As the months progressed, she slowly began to taste only certain foods with strong flavors. My attempts to assess her smelling ability began to annoy her so I slowed down. Then one day, about five months after her operation when I put a bottle of nail polish remover underneath her nose and asked her "the question" she surprised me. "Yes, mom, it smells nice." At first I was confused. Nice? Nail polish remover? But then it hit me. She said yes! She could smell! We both shrieked with joy and headed straight into the kitchen to try to find other things to smell. Approximately six months post-op it was obvious that her sense of smell was returning. This was wonderful news. She would be able to smell cookies baking, fires, flowers, stinky diapers and dead skunks!

We never found out why our daughter's feet fall asleep. It may be related to her brain malformation and it may not. We smile now when her feet fall asleep and understand that her little sleeping feet were the red herring that ultimately saved her life.

Due to the rarity of our daughter's diagnosis we live with many unanswerable questions. She is regularly followed by many different specialists and is yearly checked for spinal fluid leaks. I've gotten used to doctors saying "I don't know". No one can tell us if gravity will cause another spinal fluid leak. They cannot tell us for certain what the chances are she'll contract meningitis or if her pituitary gland will fail or if her vision will deteriorate.

Our daughter wears a medical alert bracelet which indicates her diagnosis and that she can never have an NG tube inserted in her nose.

Her brain is just too close. She cannot submerge her head underwater because that would increase her already heightened risk of meningitis. Developmental issues may arise. It's a harsh reality, but it's what I call our "new normal." Only the future knows the answers to these questions. I however, live in the present appreciating each precious moment. Tears of joy readily spill out of my eyes as I watch her accomplishments.

Without a doubt, it was the most challenging year of my life. Strange as it sounds though, I am forever grateful to my now seven year-old daughter. Through her, I learned so much about fear, acceptance, trust and the power of prayer. I now have faith in the human body's power to heal and faith in a higher power. I never could have imagined learning so many lessons in my lifetime. I feel blessed to be this special little girl's mother. Because of my daughter, I get the chance to live my life fully aware that the course I'm on can change in just one moment.

Picture Perfect

Molly Nichols

It surprises me that it can still catch me off guard, even now, after all these years. I was in the middle of an innocuous task, a long overdue cleaning of my desk drawer. Caught at the back of the drawer was a picture of a blond-haired, blue-eyed boy, sitting confidently on his small bike. The boy is two years-old, and he is gone, lost. He existed for almost three years, then he gradually disappeared. The child is my son John, who is now 16, and as different from the little boy in the picture as someone else's child would be. John will never drive a car, or go to college, or live on his own, because he is autistic.

It is human nature to engage in somewhat macabre debates. Is it better to die quickly, or to suffer from a long illness, but have time to say goodbye? If you had to pick, which sense would you lose, hearing or sight? I find myself envying other special needs mothers, who knew from the moment of birth that their child would be different. Not to say any of it is easy, quick death versus putting your house in order is still death, but at least you know what you're dealing with from the start. Again, human nature to think another road would be an easier hike; it's all uphill after all. But autism has a special cruelness when it makes its appearance, as if often does, at age one or two or three. It allows you to fall in love with your child, only to have him snatched away, You still love your child, you will always love your child fiercely, but he is different, and you have lost forever the happy baby with his delightfully doughy arms and infectious chuckle.

Like it or not, parents tend to form expectations for their children almost from the moment they are born. As parents, we almost involuntarily label our children. We know it's a bad thing to do, we resented our parents doing it to us and yet we do it. We do it in part because the differences in children are fascinating. Here are two beings with the same genetic possibilities, and yet with such markedly different personalities. My oldest son, Patrick was high maintenance from the beginning, with his wiry, dark hair and eyes showing his Hispanic roots, exhaustingly active, creative, dramatic. John, I decided after a year, was going to be my rock, the quiet, steady one. He would be the responsible guiding hand for his mercurial older brother. I could already picture him, patting my shoulder and telling me not to worry about Patrick's latest escapade.

John surveyed the world with a bemused and benign gaze, even from the infant seat. He possessed a patience Patrick would never attain. On car trips, I would glance in the rear view mirror and notice John sitting perfectly still in his car seat, blanket over his head. Lord knows how long he had been sitting there, waiting for someone to notice. When I hastily and belatedly asked, where's John?, the blanket would start to vibrate silently as John laughed delightedly underneath it. I was the envy of every mother, give that boy some Cheerios, and you could take him anywhere. From the time he could talk, he was blessed with perfect pitch — he could sing anything after hearing it once. There were many nights when I would walk by John's room long after I'd put him in his crib, and I would hear him singing to himself. When he was tired, he would lie down contentedly with his blanket held to his cheek, thumb plugged firmly in his mouth.

When we started the god-awful round of doctors, and more doctors, pediatricians, neurologists, psychologists, psychiatrists, they all insisted that there must have been some indication, some deviation, some warning bell I failed to hear. I got to the point where I would bring John's baby book with me whenever we saw a new doctor, and read those contemporaneous entries to back up my claim that there was nothing out of the norm. I don't think they ever truly believed me (I found out that with some doctors, it was as much about the mother as the child) but it gave me the reassurance that I needed to stand my ground in those horrible days. In the nightmare that life had become, they were not going to take away my sweet baby, my benevolent toddler and make me doubt that he had ever existed.

And so we limped on, until now, thirteen years later. For better or worse, to a large extent, John's course is now set. Over the years, slowly, insidiously, many things have been taken away — the normal IQ he first tested with, the ability to mainstream at school. Like his non-autistic contemporaries, John's path of development has been unpredictable, only more so. The one thing I have learned is not to even attempt to predict the future. It has not only been completely terrifying to contemplate, with all its potential pitfalls, but the present is so ever-changing, it is enough to try to keep up with today. Anne Lamott wrote once that you need not see the entire road ahead of you, you only have to see what's in your headlights. I have adopted that as a pretty good philosophy to live by.

It is my lot as John's mother to be the repository for all of his anxieties. This is in large part due to John's touching belief that there is no problem I cannot solve, no worry I cannot correct. He actually keeps a list of things that bother him, things I have to make right before he can move on to other things. The list ranges from the mundane ("It's okay if I lose computer time at school") to the worrisome ("Eating the dog's food will not hurt me."). The only acceptable answer to any of these inquiries is "Yes, it's okay." Attempts to elicit information ("Did you eat the dog's food, John?") are met with an insistent and perseverative "Say it's okay, Mommy." No spontaneous answers allowed. As John e-mailed his brother not too long ago, "Just remember, Patrick, Mommy is ALWAYS right." I can appreciate the backhanded blessing of having a sixteen year- old son who thinks I am always right and the fountain of all wisdom, but this time, I don't think there are many mothers who would envy me the whole package.

While the future is too frightening to contemplate, the past is also filled with black holes and so it is not a place I visit often. Surprisingly, it's not the moments of anguish (and believe me, there are plenty of those) that are the most painful to remember, but the moments of hope. The time when it looked like maybe it would all go away, that the little boy on his bike would miraculously rejoin us, resurrected from the autism that encased him. It seems impossible that there was ever a time when we lived without autism. It has become an ever-present lodger, the houseguest from hell that refuses to leave. I recall that time with a sense of wonder and remember how trivial some of those worries seemed, how carelessly I accepted the bounty of two healthy boys.

Autism remains the enemy and if there was a way to annihilate it, I would do it in a heartbeat. I would ruthlessly sacrifice anything short of my children's well-being to blast it out of the house. For all these years, every wish on a star, candle lit in church, longer wishbone piece pulled has been for John. There is never room for anything else. It will never change, but I will never accept it, either. I have read that when you have a special needs child it is natural to go through the classic stages of grief, I am stuck permanently somewhere between denial and anger, and I fear I will never reach acceptance. And I will never completely cease to grieve that little boy in the picture, even as I put it back in the drawer, and shut it firmly.

Eye of the Storm

Jenny Menn

It is January 4th, our 17th wedding anniversary.

Eric and I both have been mauled by a child who is not our daughter. She looks like her, but Chloe is just not around much anymore. We need to find her and let her know we love her very very much and will do whatever it takes to make her well again. She has endured months of nightmares of being attacked by dinosaurs. She has delusions no child should have to experience. It doesn't occur to me until later just how stressful her reality has been.

Chloe assumes her "other" voice just before bedtime. She is roaring and growling with hands curled, chasing Caitie, our gentle tiger cat screaming "I'm gonna get you! *I'm gonna KILL YOU. COME HEEEERE, YOU!*"

It's all we can do to both stop her, and rescue Caitie from the T-Rex's clutches, Chloe's manic-driven alter ego. This is not our daughter! In spite of the late hour, I page Dr. Graham, Chloe's psychiatrist. When she calls back I ask if she can hear Chloe in the background roaring. She can. I describe what has been happening. "I believe she is having a psychotic response to the clomipramine" Dr. Graham responds. She confirms what we already feared would be the case, that Chloe has early-onset bipolar disorder.

In the mid-1990s it is next to impossible to find information on early onset bipolar disorder. The closest reference book I could find in our town library was a tattered old tome, *Manic Depressive Insanity* and *Paranoia* by Dr. Emil Kraepelin (whom, I later learned, had first used the term manic depression). I read it to try to climb inside of Chloe's head and understand what she is seeing, feeling, hearing.

Dr. Graham repeats her recommendation of hospitalization. I tell her give us one more day. We want to think about it. If things are not better, we will call her. She wants to phone the psychiatric hospital to reserve a bed. It is a fair distance away. She assures us they are good, with a large pediatric ward staffed by compassionate professionals. "Just think of it as a weekend of rest," she adds.

The following night, once again, Eric and I take turns sleeping. Chloe is up most nights, repeatedly attacking us. She is frightened, restless, agitated, and psychotic. This has been going on for months. We sleep warily a few hours nightly. I live on adrenaline and caffeine. We cut as far back on her medicine as we safely can to wean Chloe from it.

It is 5:30 Sunday morning. During his watch in the living room, Eric falls asleep. Chloe creeps down the stairs in her flannel footsies and proceeds to viciously attack him. Somehow, she flips the glasses off his face and attacks his eyes. She claws brutally. The T-Rex is back again in full fury.

At 6:30 a.m., I come downstairs unaware of what has happened. Everything is quiet; Chloe is watching cartoons. I am making pancakes for a Sunday breakfast. Eric walks into the kitchen where I am standing, flipping pancakes, talking to me. I casually look up at his face and see he is unaware his eye is bleeding. I turn off the stove and get a compress for him and tell him to look in the mirror. He is stunned. Chloe seems unaware of anything out of the ordinary. She is watching cartoons, waiting for breakfast.

Chloe has lost all control of her impulses, her moods, and her actions.

Eric does not realize the extent of his injuries. We are sleep-deprived and attacks are becoming so randomly regular that they are now a normal part of our life.

I have to act fast. I phone Lena, Chloe's regular babysitter, a woman thoroughly attuned to Chloe's needs. I tell her that I must get Eric to the hospital. I don't say why. I know if I do, I will have to cope with more explaining than I can manage. Thankfully, Lena agrees without hesitation. My relief is immeasurable. I feed Chloe quickly, get her dressed, and drop her off on our way to the emergency room.

Eric and I are finally able to discuss our thoughts, fears, and certainty of Chloe's need for hospitalization during the ride to the hospital. We feel exhausted, drained of all energy. Although Eric has a scary looking, bloody red eye, there is no permanent damage. It is time to act. We can't risk any more injuries. We head for home.

We decide we will tell Chloe that she is going to go to a sleepover in a place with lots of other kids. Although Chloe loves sleepovers, she has had only two; both were very difficult for her. She would get overly excited and ended up frightening the other child. Chloe has never been invited to another child's house for a sleepover or anything else for that matter. Other kids clearly don't spiral out of control the way she does. It is hard for them to comprehend her behaviors and responses to life around her.

When we get home from the ER, I pack Chloe's clothes as Eric makes the intake arrangements with the hospital. He then drives to Lena's to pick her up. The patch on Eric's eye fascinates her. She begins to caress his face as she examines, without guile, guilt, or realization of the damage she has done. She seems absolutely fine now, making our decision that much harder.

We cannot waiver however, because we know what's around the next corner. As we predicted, Chloe is excited about the sleepover. Her joy makes us feel guilty and ashamed. She packs her favorite pillow, her toys, and her beloved plastic T-Rex.

After a quick dinner, we load her little pink Miss Kitty sleepover suit-case into the car and begin the long drive to the hospital. It is completely dark now, which only seems to add to the horror of what we are doing.

We arrive after an exhausting drive, turning into a long, winding entrance road lined with trees. Driving up to the huge mansion-like hospital, we go into admitting, pillow and stuffies in hand; Chloe wearing her pajamas. She plays on the floor distractedly, but seems oddly happy. I leave Eric with her and go into another room. It takes me a while to explain to the nurse exactly what has been going on. The nurse scribbles into her pad and nods.

A painful battery of questions about mood, affect and behavior are followed by endless forms to be signed. Finally it is time to escort Chloe to the children's ward. We enter through a heavy steel door that locks behind us. The unit has a long hallway with rooms off each side. There is a recreation room with some books, toys, and a television. We sign additional paperwork and are asked more questions.

After a doctor briefly examines her, the admission is complete. For now she will have her own room for observation. It is after midnight.

Chloe is hugging her pillow, tired, but still a little wired. An aide (with all the charm of a prison warden) tells us that we need to leave now, so she can settle in.

Eric hugs Chloe and tells her that he loves her and will see her tomorrow. I do the same and find I cannot let her go. I continue to hug her. For the first time in what seems like years, she hugs me back. Deliberately.

I am trying not to cry. I am trying not to feel like a failure. How could we leave such a tiny, helpless child in here? What would happen to her now? Would they take her away from us for failing to keep her sane? Most importantly, how would Chloe manage emotionally here? Would this experience make her feel damaged somehow?

I can't bear it. The more I think, the harder it becomes. I am still locked in an embrace when the aide, waiting impatiently by the door tells me "You're not helping her if you stay there." I am beside myself with grief, furious at the insensitivity of the aide. I am frightened to leave her there, looking smaller than ever. "We'll see you tomorrow, love," we tell her, and walk back through the heavy steel door. As it locks behind us, we continue silently down the hallway, and into the cold night. I feel lost, empty.

I am thinking she will be here for a day or two. It is almost three weeks before she is discharged and back home again. This is only a first chapter of many more to come. It is January 6th, "Family Day." It is the day we celebrate both Chloe's adoption and becoming a family. Happy Family Day, indeed.

Chloe had just turned five when first hospitalized. Before the age of 10, she would suffer mania, psychosis, and violence so extreme she would be hospitalized three more time; participate in approximately 25 medication trials; attend two different specialized schools that proved unable to serve her needs; a residential school placement when she was 10 in which she stayed for a year and a half. We learned much over the year; particularly from a pair of gifted therapists at her residential school who helped all of us learn new ways to manage, talk about, and cope with difficult times.

An MRI performed in 2000 showed that Chloe was born with clearly visible mid-brain abnormalities affecting her learning abilities, sensory, emotional, social, and executive function skills. Also, due to a very thin corpus callosum (the membrane separating the brain's hemispheres), the left and right functions of her brain are in continual conflict.

Today, she is 15, attending a wonderful high school in a specialized setting. She's doing well. Because of Chloe's fierce spirit, Eric and I do not rule out any possibility for her. She may well need to live in a specialized group home, or some type of assisted-living situation. We will deal with that when the time is at hand.

For now, we'll take it just one day at a time.

A Mother's Instinct

Ann M. Curtis

Call it mother's instinct, but I always knew something was different with my daughter. Right from the beginning, I sensed that she was unique.

Born healthy, Caitlin's APGAR scores were fine and we had no reason to worry that anything was less than perfect with her. She refused to breastfeed, though, and I had to change my expectations and begin bottle-feeding. Jaundice made a hospital stay under the "blazing beach lights" necessary and fifteen ear infections before she was five months-old kept us hopping.

Health issues aside, we were thankful to have such an easy baby. She ate well, slept through the night at four months and was generally a fun-loving and happy baby. In the beginning, we assumed that there was nothing about her that was out of the ordinary.

That year she turned two, everything changed. She went from a size 2T to a 6X and wanted to eat constantly. She didn't have much intelligible/decipherable speech and the tantrums started. She would cry over just about anything. And that cry! It was a high-pitched scream that would set our teeth on edge.

We started having problems getting her to bed and getting her dressed. Moving her from the crib to the bed was a major challenge.

If we pushed her too hard about anything, she would throw a fit.

At the time, my husband and I both worked outside the home and getting Caitlin ready and off to daycare was extremely stressful Eventually, Caitlin's problems became so overwhelming that I lost my job.

I know now that Caitlin will be our only child and that only children tend to have different personality traits than those with siblings. Being first time parents, we tried to convince ourselves that we were overly anxious and that everything Caitlin was doing was a normal part of development. But that darn mother's intuition told me that something wasn't quite right. That something was called Sensory Processing Dysfunction.

Since Caitlin's body doesn't register when she is full, she is constantly hungry, hence the weight gain. From the time she was a baby, Caitlin has always been off the charts in the height and weight categories for her age. As she grew older, we were unable to hold or carry her for long periods of time; she was too tall and too heavy. This was hard for her to understand. She quickly outgrew her stroller, which was especially difficult since she tires easily and doesn't have much energy. Her weight is an issue that we continue to grapple with.

Raising a special needs child means that I rarely have time to myself. I miss it dearly. Caitlin does not understand the concept of personal space. She is very needy and always wants someone close by. It used to be I couldn't be anywhere in the room but right next to her. With time, that has improved; I can now be in a different room and sometimes even on a different floor. On any given day, her mood and neediness dictates how much time alone I will be allowed.

Caitlin tries so hard to please us, and most of the time, she's a wonderful kid. Thanks to some therapy, she is getting to know herself better and is usually able to articulate when she is having a bad day. She'll say, "I don't know why my body is doing this," or "my brain and body don't work together or listen to each other," or "I'm stupid" (Which is usually followed by her hitting herself on the head).Temper tantrums can now be tempered and even stopped before they begin by watching for warning signs We don't catch every one, but the amount and severity has decreased.

However, when she does become overwhelmed or anxious, she is not rational and will often have a fit, crying and running away to hide. Because of this, I live most of my days stressed and sleep deprived. Stressed from Caitlin's never-ending demands and sleep deprived due to the multiple tasks I do everyday.

Caitlin wasn't diagnosed with SPD until she was five years-old although she had several interventions before that. Nowhere along the way did anyone mention or diagnose Caitlin with SPD, and it wasn't until we took her to a childhood specialist and I did my own research, that we were finally able to diagnose Caitlin and get her the help she needed.

SPD is known as a silent or hidden disability and obtaining a diagnosis can be a frustrating battle. We know that the best thing we can do for her is to wait and hope that along the way her emotional maturity will grow with her. I have no doubt that she will reach this point, but since she is nowhere near self-regulation it seems like a long way away.

Like most parents of special needs children, my husband and I sometimes wonder what our lives would be like if we didn't have Caitlin.

Since we married later in life and already had our own hobbies and interests, the decision to have children was not made lightly. After Caitlin's birth, we made the tough decision not to have any other children. I've always wanted more, but taking care of Caitlin is like taking care of three children. Neither my husband or I are able or willing to put up with the stress more would bring, able or willing to put up with the stress of raising more than one.

We moved only two years before Caitlin was born, so our friendship support network is not very strong. Caitlin's condition decides what we do and where we go and her mood dictates just how much she can handle. She can have a fabulous day one day and a totally rotten one the next. There is no consistency.

Caitlin's need to be in control is hard for other children. Caitlin has a hard time just playing like normal children play, with give and take and back and forth. Her bossiness is her way of trying to keep order and take charge when she herself doesn't feel very much in control of herself.

Kids have a hard time understanding and knowing how to respond when Caitlin gets upset, cries, or throws a tantrum. Because of this, most of them tend to shy away from her. This hurts her tremendously and we work hard to keep her self-esteem healthy.

Caitlin can be very hard on herself, saying she's dumb and stupid and doesn't know anything. Living in the country where there aren't many children her age necessitates that we need to set up play dates which takes a lot of advance planning and thought.

We've tried to compensate for many of these things by having pets who, we hope, help Caitlin to learn how to get along with others, share and empathize.

Caitlin knows she is different or, as she likes to say, special. In fact, she's the one who kept telling us her brain and body wouldn't work together. Caitlin's greatest difficulties lie in her doubting herself, which can do a number on her self-esteem.

She needs lots of encouragement learning to control her volatile emotions and feelings. She also needs lots of help learning social skills. But she is artistic and has a thirst for knowledge. She has a gorgeous laugh and smile. Caitlin really is a beautiful person.

I worry about the future. Will she be able to function on her own? Will she make friends? Will she have a boyfriend? What will puberty be like for her? Like other parents, we don't know what the future holds. But, with guidance, love, patience, and understanding, we're going to help Caitlin be all she can be. After all, isn't that what parents are for?

The Rules of Engagement

Diane Eaton

"No child of mine is going to be an ABA robot!" That's what I said during my research after I learned that my child had Pervasive Developmental Disorder Not Otherwise Specified ("PDD-NOS"), which is one of several Autism Spectrum Disorders. My husband and I read articles in scholarly journals, books, and parents' stories on the Internet. This very strong feeling was certainly not based on any experience with this program. It was based on a fear that ABA (Applied Behavioral Analysis) would only treat my child's behavior and not bother at all to deal with the psychology at work behind the behavior.

I imagined my little boy at the dinner table saying to us "What did you do today?" exactly as he had been taught by his therapists in the monotone of those who know what they're saying but not why they're saying it and not even caring about the answer. The only reason they're asking the question is that they have learned the basics of what people say in certain social situations, but not caring at all about the feelings or lives of the people with which they're socializing. I also found out that this therapy came with cost. The children were forced to say and do what they were told whether they wanted to or not. This, of course, would fuel many a tantrum throughout the day. How cruel is it to force onto children what you could coax out of them, right?

I liked the idea of "floor time," which is otherwise known as the Greenspan method. This seemed so much more natural and conducive to real fun and a love of learning. At this time, David was a little over two years-old and had three words in his vocabulary. The words changed every month or two, meaning that he was replacing words instead of adding them. It hurt my heart every time I heard him start to say "gud" (his word for dog) but no longer heard him say "door." He had yet to say "Mommy."

David was a part of New Jersey's Early Intervention Program, which at the time offered a few hours a week of developmental intervention and speech and occupational therapies. But, the problem was, none of it was working. In fact, his vocabulary had gone down from three words to no words and the rest of the world was starting to become little more than wallpaper. He was turning into a zombie.

We finally found a wonderful diagnostician who encouraged us to try ABA. She personally knew a very talented programmer who she trusted implicitly. When Laura came to assess David, my husband and I were ready to give her our list of David's strengths and weaknesses. She didn't take the paper from us. "I don't need that. When I'm done I'll tell you what his strengths and weaknesses are,"she said. Already, she was a breath of fresh air, albeit a bit direct. During his assessment, she was rewarding positive behavior and correct answers with verbal praise and his favorite foods and toys. Anytime he tried to get away from the table, she put his hands on him and kept him there until he quieted down and was ready to follow her directions again. I'd never seen such tantrums from him before. They didn't seem to faze her. As upsetting as it was to me, I could see that she wasn't hurting him so I let her continue. After about an hour she talked to us about ABA and autism in general and the toll this kind of therapy would take on us. She wasn't going to accept David as a client if we weren't willing to jump in with both feet. Nothing else was working; how could we say no?

She started our training immediately, showing us how to get him to listen and follow simple directions around the house. He was terrific for the first couple of weeks and I thought, "Hey, this is working; it's not so tough." Laura warned me that this was the honeymoon period. Once David got a clue that this was going to become a permanent part of his life, things changed very quickly.

While she was at our house again for more training, David was refusing to listen to me. I had told him to "give me the book," something he'd done before and was not confused about in the least. His consequence was to have me do it with him, my hands over his, over and over until he chose to do it himself. He screamed, he threw the book, he kicked at me and hit me. Laura suggested bringing him to the corner and having him sit and stand over and over until he did it quietly and then we could go back to working on the book. I was sitting him down and standing him up for about half an hour and my back was hurting, but not as much as my heart. Why was he doing this? It was simple; sit, stand, give me a book. We weren't asking him to recite Shakespeare! Laura took over for a while because he was definitely still intimidated by her at this point. Once she got compliance from him, she would give him over to me and have him mind me, too. She sat him down and stood him up and his screaming reached such a pitch that I ran into the bathroom and cried silently so that David wouldn't hear me (although, who was I kidding, he wouldn't have heard a fire engine over the noise he was making!).

I cried and cried thinking, "Why am I letting this woman make my child scream? What's the point? Is this really going to help him talk, look at other people when they spoke to him, or want to play with another child? Why am I letting her do this to my baby?" The mother bear in me wanted to throw her out of my house. But another thought came to me as clear as a bell; if I did that, my son would still be autistic and I still wouldn't know how to help him. I calmed myself down and resolved to try again. Then I heard something different from outside the bathroom door. At first I thought I was hearing things, but then I heard it again. His crying was quieter and he was saying "Mommy."

Once Laura was able to get him to sit and stand on his own she said, "Ok, David, now you're going to do it for Mommy." It took another fifteen minutes but he did it, and then we went back to the book and he finally did that, too. I gave him such praise and took him in my arms, hugging him so hard I thought he would burst. Laura told me she was dying to give him to me right after he said it, but she knew we had to finish what we started first or else he would learn that he could get out of anything just by saying Mommy. Laura put together a data sheet for me of some simple but crucial skills David had to have before he could move on to learning anything else. I became his first therapist and worked with him imitation of hand and body movements and how to identify objects and pictures by pointing, giving, and touching. It was the hardest work I have ever done in my life and one direction took about three hours. Soon after, David started using words to identify or ask for things. They were just nouns but David was talking! I called the whole family and we were all crying.

David is five years-old now and he's attending a regular kindergarten class with an ABA therapist shadowing him. He'll also have some

ABA therapy at home in order to work on the trouble spots at school both socially and academically. We learned that he is quite intelligent. He knows all his letters and their sounds and can count easily up to thirty and even fifty if he tries really hard. He knows all the planets in our solar system and how a caterpillar turns into a butterfly, and that's only the tip of the iceberg!

I know he'll never truly be cured, but I can tell you he's come such a long way since the beginning. He can have rudimentary conversation and talk on the phone for a few minutes. Of course, when he learns a social initiation or conversation for the first time, it is a bit robotic and eye contact is always an issue to some degree. The difference is that when he's done it enough times outside of therapy, there is inflection to it and he understands what he's saying and why he's saying it. He recently sang "Happy Birthday" to my sister on the phone with all of the inflection that you would expect from a child his age. She was overjoyed! It's still a tough job but everything we do has its rewards and it's consequences. The big reward for us is that we've come down from the wallpaper and have the beginnings of a real relationship with our son.

Only Time Will Tell

Erika Dahlquist

"That poor little guy." "Yeah, he's such a little trooper." I say, as I secretly think to myself, NO! Poor ME. Ever try being the one to nebulize a toddler? Wrestle him to force-feed medication? Go to speech therapy and immunologists on TOP of all the other stuff that comes with having a toddler? Alex looks up at me and smiles. I melt. After my mental tirade, the guilt trip begins. I'm being selfish, I tell myself. He has had a tough time and it could be so much worse. I didn't expect this parenting thing to be easy. Stop whining.

As my poor little guy makes a beeline for the swings, I chat with my best friend who has two children under three years-old. We talk about all the typical mom things. "Brady started refusing to eat anything that isn't brown," she says. "Breaded vegetables?" I offer. "Hmmm... not a bad idea," she agrees. It's easy to fill the conversation with the typical "mom with a toddler topics," food, tantrums, sleep deprivation.

I watch her little boy and little girl play together. So cute. One of each. I think to myself "I just can't do it again". I barely survived Alex's first year. Could I handle it better knowing what I know now? Would it be easier the second time around? Chances are that I'd have a perfectly healthy baby. Can I take that chance? What if my second child has the same or even more problems? These questions haunt me.

I always wanted three kids,that was my plan. Now, I laugh at the idea I had a plan before I knew what raising kids really entailed, much less a child with a developmental disorder, primary immunodeficiency and several other health issues.

Our families have no history of any of Alex's health issues. His health problems were so subtle and surfaced one at a time. A sneak attack would be an accurate description. Together these issues overwhelmed my husband and me. I laugh and play with Alex during the day and I cry myself to sleep at night as I worry about what raising a child with autism will mean.

We are lucky to have such a good early childhood development program in our area. It was a mixed blessing when they called and told us we qualified for free services. As I play with him I try to find little signs to convince myself that he really can't be autistic. But it's gotten harder and harder to deny that there's a problem, especially when I see him around other kids his age that are talking and playing with each other.

Alex's smile can light up any room. His laugh is contagious. But he's always much happier playing by himself like he's doing right now in the sand by the slide where he is organizing the rocks. That's my boy.

I hear a scream from across the playground as my friend Jodie's daughter screams for her, calling, "Momma!" As she gets ready to leave, I look over at Alex. My heart aches. I have yet to hear him call for me. I still have a really hard time talking with anyone about Alex's developmental issues. They try and cheer me up or convince me it's nothing by saying that he'll probably just grow out of it. It's a phase. He's really not that far behind. Boys take longer to communicate than girls. My uncle didn't talk until he was four and now he has a PhD. I have heard it all.

Time is the enemy to me now. Alex's diagnosis is a waiting game. Since he's just under two, he still seems like a pretty normal kid to the outside observer. I'm not sure what to expect in the future. I'm a mom. I want to protect him from all those mean people out there. But, in truth, he'll probably never notice the looks or care what other people think. I'm just angry and afraid that I'll see it. I'll notice it. I'll care.

Emergence

Shannon Andreson

I'll always remember the day in January that I betrayed my only child. I had stood watching him eat his lunch, so innocent and completely unaware as I listed my concerns to the woman at the hotline. I looked away as I continued the list and moved into the other room, desperate that he not hear me.

"He's lost words he's mastered. He's not building a vocabulary. He has an unusually long attention span. Sometimes, it's hard to get his attention," I told her. As I looked at Henry happily stuffing his mouth with peas, I couldn't believe I was having this conversation. One month shy of his second birthday, my son was blonde, brown-eyed and charming. He was perfect. He was beautiful. What was I doing?

That phone call began a new life for me and my family. A life that now includes Autism Spectrum Disorder. It was the day I officially admitted something was wrong. I'd done the research. I knew Henry showed some signs, just not a lot of them. Despite family and professionals telling me to "wait and see," assuring me Henry was fine, I knew he was different from other kids.

I am drawn to people who defy convention, but the more I read, the more I suspected that his quirks were not entirely harmless. So I stepped off the roller coaster ride and called the hotline. When I hung up, my hands shook, and I felt nauseous. Somewhere, mothers who question their child's perfection are punished. Somewhere, they are publicly revealed as cold, heartless traitors. I felt alone and utterly vulnerable.

Despite my feelings, I made the appointment. After the school team came to evaluate him and after the tests and meetings and worry and denial, we got a label of PDD-NOS. We haven't had the party yet, but we're welcoming autism into our life. We're also recognizing its unique manifestation in our son and at the same time, we're beginning to realize that he isn't a label. The stories we've heard and read are not his story. We're creating our own version of life on the spectrum. And, most days, we're doing it remarkably well.

Although I've done my research and I am not surprised by what his therapists tell me, nothing can prepare a mother for grieving the loss of a child who still lives in her home. It's the kind of grief that blindsides you when a Hallmark commercial comes on. One where the boy grows up playing ball and graduates from college.

I thought I had no expectations for my son. I refused to start a college fund, because I didn't want to place that expectation on him. He could be a carpenter like his grandfather, a drifter/hippie like his uncle, or a physicist like his father. Whatever he wanted to do was fine with me. But this diagnosis slaps me in the face with the little expectations I do have. The ones that other parents don't even recognize. I expected my wonderful son would play catch with his dad out in the backyard. I expected that he'd run wild at the playground, trying all the equipment, climbing, sliding, swinging. I expected that we'd talk about everything. I'd show the world to him, pointing out fascinating sights, and he'd attend to my words. He'd absorb my knowledge, and it would spark his imagination. And I expected all this to happen naturally, without any therapy or intervention. That's not our life. I see that life all around us, on television and on the playground. Now I know we're on a different time table. We're in a different world. I expect that my son will do all these things, but they'll happen later, and we'll have to work hard to make them happen. So I grieve those little things we have to work so hard for.

Things have always come easily to me and if I don't do something well, I simply stop doing it. It's a pattern I learned in childhood and it's stuck in my adult life. With autism, I can't quit even though it's hard. Few skills come easily to my son, and he's the one thing I'll never quit. So now I'm learning new patterns, breaking a cycle. We work hard every day. He, more than me. And we rejoice in such small things. A turn of his head to follow a pointed finger. Following through to pick up the intended object. Going up the stairs on his own and sliding down an unfamiliar slide. Greeting his dad after a day of work and saying good bye to his best friend before she's halfway down the street. These are all triumphs, and we celebrate them as such, sometimes with tears in our eyes.

Through all these tests and therapists and therapies, my son has maintained his core personality. He is a sweet, caring boy who is quick to smile and quick to laugh. He's a nurturer, like his father, and smart, very smart. As his language emerges, we learn daily how much he's absorbed from us. I've learned that those cardinals and bunny tracks I pointed to last winter weren't ignored. They were experienced, just in a way I failed to recognize. He is absorbing everything I say and show him, even though the spark is beneath the surface. And, slowly, day by day, I am learning to draw it out.

Puzzled

Jessica Thompson

It's rather difficult to determine exactly when I knew that my son was "abnormal". I suppose my awareness that my journey through parenthood would prove more treacherous than expected; a puzzle whose pieces progressively fit together, was a gradual one.

I can appreciate the fact that my son is very unique; he possesses many exceptional qualities. He is delightful and has a goofy sense of humor. He loves to dance and to entertain people with his silliness. He is compassionate, intriguing and at times impressive with his awareness and intellect. He does not cease to surprise those who know him with his absorption of the world. Unfortunately, I'll probably never know how intelligent he is or exactly what is occurring inside his head.

In contrast, at times his poor concentration, attention span and memory can be overwhelmingly frustrating. Homework is a struggle for both of us. Although I feel terrible admitting it, I have had to lower my expectations of him. I don't want to sell him short, but he is certainly incapable of completing the tasks expected of him as a first grade student. His speech is delayed and he cannot articulate his thoughts, not even his own name. As a result, I have developed a surprising ability to translate his messages, his attempts to communicate what is occurring within, unlike anyone else close to him.

He has endured many struggles in his short life. When he was three years-old, he had all but a few of his teeth removed as a result of severe damage. He had ground them down to merely bits of matter. His sensory integration issues worked against him during attempts to build relationships. He complained when I washed his hair; the sensory input was literally painful for him. He has been on seizure medication for years after enduring a 24-hour EKG and many MRI's. After three years of failed attempts, he finally was toilet trained when he was almost five years-old.

My son was born very small, weak and mild. He would not eat on his own for the first few weeks of his life. He was quiet, pleasant and responsive; yet never cried. When he was upset he'd merely make a face, as if he was crying, yet there was no sound. He was not vocal until about nine months of age when he consistently babbled. He began to say words in the following months yet then appeared to regress. Language was not the only obvious delay in his development. His gross motor skills have always been delayed; he supported his own weight, stood, crawled and walked late. In hindsight, he exhibited deficits in his social skills as well although initially I thought his lack of interest in other children was due to shyness. His sensory integration issues worked against him when he was trying (or I was trying) to help him build relationships. Once, on a play date, the other child began screaming and my son ran for the door; he could not endure the sound of the child's cries. I recall this incident as one of my earliest acknowledgements that he was unusual.

A most painfully awkward display of his deficits occurred when he was a year and a half old and we attended a "playmate's" first birthday party. He was excited to attend; he loved to be outside and to observe other children. He had just learned to walk and he fell down several times that day. I felt so many emotions seeing him fall time and time again with no obvious reason. I felt ashamed, embarrassed, frustrated, and deeply saddened. I felt the stares of other parents as they noticed his obvious difficulties. At one point, he slid from a park bench and planted his face in the cement, crying loudly. I don't know which one of us was more disturbed. As I attempted to calm him, another mother at the party insisted upon displaying her ignorance as she snidely remarked, "He doesn't get out much, does he?" Her ignorance enraged me. I felt volcanic; I wanted to say a million things, to scream, to cry and to explode. I said nothing.

It was probably at that moment that I recognized that such ignorance, such judgment would persist in my son's life, increasingly so as he aged and his differences and limitations became more evident. I realized that my son was not only at risk of being criticized by his peers but also by insensitive adults. I became aware that my son's differences were in full view for the world to see and as a result my heart would forever remain vulnerable and unprotected from the outside world.

As time went on, his difficulties multiplied. It was obvious that my baby was unique but I didn't know to what extent. I had no diagnosis, no "label" and no conception of what his future could or most likely could not be. When he was two years-old, we visited a developmental psychologist due to mounting concerns about his delays. As a result of research, I knew what speculation and possible diagnosis existed prior to and during our visit but it was not until the professional stated her observations and made an initial diagnosis that I woke up. I woke from a degree of denial to acknowledge that my son existed on the autism spectrum. I left that doctor's office completely devastated; I sobbed the entire way home from the visit and nobody muttered a word. I began a grieving process that day that still remains a struggle.

Any emotional progress that I have made is not easily evident to the outside world. While venting about general life stressors to a great friend recently, I realized that the message I am conveying to those around me is that I am still very much unable to accept our reality. It was difficult to hear my friend's words as he explained that I still needed to come to terms with the fact that I am the mother of a special needs child and I cried at his frank observations.

My relationships with many of my friends have been affected as a result of my son's diagnosis, although only of my own creation. I believe I've erected an emotional wall; I've attempted to protect my son and my own emotions from any perceived threat of criticism. Consequently, I have isolated myself even from those I care about. I rarely visit friends of nearly 20 years who also have children. Witnessing my son's struggle to communicate with and relate to the other children is physically painful. I remain heartbroken.

I also find it difficult to relate to other parents and it becomes obvious at the dreaded playground. I experience much discomfort as my son's curiosity for and interest in his peers peaks and his failure to communicate and keep up with them is unavoidable. When he attempts to play with other children his poor social skills, speech and motor skill ability quickly discourage much of an interaction. As proud parents watch their toddlers traverse a bridge on the playground equipment, I hold onto my six year-old son's hand as he struggles to stabilize himself and successfully utilize his muscles. It is in this setting that I observe his awareness that he *is* unlike the other children. I attempt not to cry as my chest aches for him and find myself fantasizing about having a typically developing child.

Although I believe my son notices that he is atypical, it is difficult to determine to what extent. He has not expressed his observations, frustrations or any awareness of his disability yet, but I realize that does not indicate a lack of his perception. The fact that he receives front door service from the school bus is a luxury he believes all children receive. I am hesitant to emphasize the fact that he is "special". I would hate for him to use his disability as a crutch, an excuse not to perform to the best of his ability, or even worse, to use it for manipulation. I am concerned about placing limitations on him and also about damaging his self-confidence and self-worth. However, I don't want him to get disillusioned either.

Thoughts of my son's future make me paralyzed with anxiety. When I consider the possibilities, I am extremely nervous, frightened and confused. I know my role, I understand the many positions I must fill in order to successfully address the duty which has been thrust upon me. However, I am unsure about my ability to do so and I must constantly evade such doubts. The idea of leaving my son behind to face the cruel world and so many hurdles scares me unlike anything else. The thought of someone stealing his innocence and taking advantage of his sweet nature greatly worries me as well.

My son has made much progress and continues to do so. Nevertheless, we undeniably have an extensive journey ahead of us. Preparing him to face the world will prove to be a daunting task. I must instruct him on so many topics, including a most disheartening chore of identifying and tackling discrimination. To make matters more challenging, I must do so while attempting to preserve his warm, friendly nature. Teaching him to be cautious of the evils of society while not instilling an all-encompassing fear will be quite complicated.

Although I expect that we will endure much frustration and potential heartache, I know that we will experience much joy as well. My son is the inspiration for much happiness in our family, and I believe he will further satisfy that role in our lives. He has already taught me to develop traits that have not come easy such as patience and selflessness. I imagine that he and I will continue to learn and grow together. Carrying out this mission will never prove effortless and I must constantly pursue strength and optimism in order to persevere. I have found that strength exists much closer to home than I expected. When I have practically drowned in tears as a result of my despair, my son has stroked my hair, wiped my eyes and comforted me with, "It's okay Mommy".

A Difficult Journey

Renee Bryant

In the beginning, one of the most difficult aspects of being a mother of a special needs child was getting a diagnosis. I found it unnerving to see the pediatrician every two weeks with a screaming baby only to be told that my infant son had another ear infection. From the time he was three weeks-old until his second birthday, we saw several pediatricians and almost every time we were handed a prescription for antibiotics.

Shawn cried inconsolably and often. Nothing seemed to calm him except for a ride in the car with loud rock and roll music. He would finally give in and sleep, until the car shut off in the driveway. I can chuckle about that now because we ended up leaving the car running in the driveway, be damned if anyone stole it. We wanted our baby to sleep so we could rest ourselves. After tucking him back into his bed, my husband would go outside and turn it off.

Just before Shawn's second birthday, I finally broke down. I spent three days journaling Shawn's every movement. I went on the Internet at night after he was in bed and checked out a few of my own suspicions and found that he fit the profile of an autistic child. I could honestly go down a list of behaviors that I found and check off eleven out of fourteen. And, that was being generous, in reality, there were probably more.

I took my journal to the doctor and proceeded to read my scribbles while he observed Shawn's behaviors and scratched his head. He looked at me and asked me what I thought. My response was swift. I told him I thought Shawn was autistic and that no one wanted to tell me. He looked at me sadly and said, "I think you're right."

There were no sirens blaring, no bells ringing and yet in my own head I felt like cymbals were crashing in around me. I opened my mouth and nothing came out. I was sucking in air and the tears began to fall. The fight was over. My baby was imperfect and I felt like it was all my fault. How could I go home and tell my husband that his only child was never going to be okay? I couldn't even imagine telling our families or our friends. We were not a welcome sight at most of our friends and family's homes because of Shawn's screaming and crying. But now? Was everyone going to pity us. I didn't want their sympathy. I had enough sorrow in my own heart and soul. I needed answers that no one could give me. More than that, I needed hope.

Telling Shawn's dad was quite difficult. He would take in a tidbit of information and then he would deny it, seemingly wishing it away. I know that deep down he did believe it, but could not bear to admit it to himself.

Our parents had different ways of dealing with the news. My husband, Kurt's parents, would not accept it. They refused to see anything different about Shawn and would constantly point out anything Shawn did that was normal. Part of me resented them for not accepting his diagnosis, but another part of me was glad that they thought he was so normal. My parents on the other hand accepted it like it was old news. My mother was present when I gave birth to Shawn and she said she knew there was something wrong with him the moment he came out. That angered me and hurt me. How could she have possibly known that? He didn't look any different than any other infant.

Shawn was my fifth child and my husband's first and only child. Shawn's father had no idea that he had missed any landmarks in his development. Since he had no experience with infants, Shawn's crying, while annoying, was not a red flag to him. He thought that he was just a fussy baby. But the red flags were flying for me. I think the one thing that really struck me and hurt was that all my other children would look at my face lovingly and adoringly when they were nursing. Shawn looked right through me as if I wasn't there. He nursed like a wild animal leaving scratches and bruises. There was no bonding on his end. I feared he was blind until I noticed his eyes tracking a moving object. He loved to watch things spin.

By the time Shawn could raise a fist, sometime before his first birthday, he would punch or slap his dad or myself in the face hard enough to bring tears. He had rage that we couldn't seem to control. My parents thought that I wouldn't live to raise a child like Shawn and thought it might be best if I made him a ward of the state. This tore my heart out and it took me years to get over the hurt that statement caused. Shawn is not disposable. He is my gift and even though he isn't what I expected, God trusted me with him for a reason. The subject came up again a few years later with an apology from my mother.

Since I was 37 when Shawn was born, I worried about what would happen to Shawn when I died. Who would take care of him? Suddenly, 37 seemed much too old to have a baby. I had no guarantee that I would live to see him into old age. It was a gut wrenching thought..

Part of Shawn's difficulty was his sensitivity to light, sound and touch. He could hear a plane coming a full minute before we ever heard or saw it in the sky. The simple hum of a neon light bulb would cause him great emotional distress. Understanding these issues helped us avoid exposing him to certain situations, and if we couldn't avoid something, at least we knew why he was having a meltdown. We put sunglasses on him and kept them on even when we went into stores so the bright lights wouldn't disturb him. He also liked them because he didn't like people looking directly into his eyes and having them on made him feel more comfortable. We used ear muffs, the kind that are used as ear protection at a shooting range so we could take him outside because even the sounds of buzzing insects would send him screaming into the house. Finding solutions for his issues was much easier than figuring out each issue. Little by little, we discovered ways that he enjoyed being touched and held and when he came to us for affection on his own, it was milestone. We took joy in the simplest accomplishments and at the same time realized that we had missed so much with the other children. Life became more enjoyable with each passing day.

I didn't have to look hard to find out that Shawn has an amazing memory. I was determined to make that work for him. One of my biggest joys was teaching Shawn to read when he was three. I used magnetic poetry and taught him to sight read right on the refrigerator. I used the word magnets with magnets that matched. For the word boy, I had a Bam Bam Rubble magnet (from the Flintstones) and then placed the word magnet "Boy" under it and so on. It was fun and Shawn caught on very quickly. Shawn learned to read before he could hold a conversation, opening a way of communicating that I never thought possible. Now that Shawn could read, he began to express himself which made him less angry. The tantrums and meltdowns became less frequent. We began to understand each other. Each passing day, as he learned to read new words, his communication skills soared.

Shawn is eight years-old now. It has been an incredible journey to this point. We have overcome many obstacles. He no longer needs sunglasses or ear protection to go outside and even when you look at him closely, you cannot tell that he has any issues. Early intervention worked well for him. Medically, there isn't anything that can be done. There is no one answer for these special children. I had to look through Shawn's eyes to find many of the answers I needed to be an effective parent.

I believe that I am a better parent after having a special needs child. I see things much differently and the emphasis is on the positive things with him and the other children. I have learned to make snap decisions about what is really important and what can be let go. This has served me well with all of my children. I have had to reinvent myself as a parent and it changed how I parent all of my children.

I have learned to appreciate differences in myself and others. As a family, we don't define ourselves by our differences, we embrace them. I stopped trying to push a square peg through a round hole. I learned that if I broadened the opening the peg will slide right in and even if it isn't a perfect fit love can fill many gaps.

A Letter to my Son

Chelsea Celentano

Dear Santino,

There is so much I want you to know about how I feel about you, about how much you mean to me. I began loving you long before you were born, long before I felt you kick and tumble, long before I saw that "grain of rice" on the ultrasound screen.

I loved you years before that, when you were a dream, a perfect little miracle in my mind. Your daddy was away on business a lot, so many nights I'd lie awake and think about all the great things we were going to do together, all of the things I was going to teach you. I couldn't wait to hear your first word, and sometimes I would try to guess what it would be. Of course, I secretly hoped it would be "Mommy", but just hearing your voice would be enough for me. I pictured us going for walks together and watching your face as you discovered all the new and exciting things the world had in store for you. I know I was getting way ahead of myself, but I also thought about your distant future. Would you be a football star, would you have a lot of friends, what college would you go to, who would you marry? The list was endless. I would go to weddings and watch a mother dance with her son and I'd hold my belly and think, "Someday, this will be us."

When you were born, it was the most beautiful moment of my life. Every part of you was perfect, and I couldn't wait to hold you and look into those eyes of yours and tell you how loved you were. There is something so special about the first time a mother holds her child, that instant when a connection is made. It came immediately for us. You were my son and I was your mother, and at that moment, no one else in the world existed.

Fast forward six months to you smiling, laughing, cooing, sitting up on your own, trying to crawl. Every day you amazed us with something new. You would make a sound and Daddy and I would try and figure out if a word was coming. You were all over the place, crawling and pulling yourself up on everything by eight months, and one week after you turned 10 months, you were off and running, literally We thought it was only a matter of time before the talking would start, before you would say, "Da Da" and "Ma Ma". At a year old, you said your first word, "Okay." It was the first and only time you said it.

It's true that a mother knows her child like no other person in the world. Your Daddy loves you more than he loves anyone, but I know you like nobody else. So when I started to notice little things, like how you wouldn't look at anyone when they called your name, or how you didn't point to anything, I became instantly sick. Of course there were many people who told me I was being ridiculous, but I knew. In my heart, I knew. Now I know this is going to sound strange to you, but somewhere deep down, I knew long before I saw any signs. When I was pregnant, I used to hear this little voice that would say, "This one is special. He's not like the other kids. He's different." Please don't think I'm crazy. I just believe it was God's way of telling me what was in store for us.

After a while, you didn't really make eye contact with anyone, and even though you were a very happy toddler, you would tantrum for any big or small thing that seemed frustrating to you. And then there was the talking, or lack of it, I should say. You said nothing. Some babbling, but no words. When Daddy or I would come home from work, you didn't even acknowledge that we were in the room, and that hurt us so badly. The one thing that has always remained, however, which I am so grateful for, is that you have always loved hugging, and kissing, and cuddling with us. Being able to hold you and tell you how much we loved you meant (and still means) the world to us. I remember saying your prayers with you every night, and I'd give you big hugs and always end by asking God to let you know that we were ready to listen when you were ready to talk. It still gives me chills when I think about it.

At your 18 month check-up, the doctor told me I was worrying for no reason, but one month later I was back in that office getting the phone numbers I needed to figure out what was going on with you. Your eye contact had gotten worse, and I wasn't wasting any more time. Early Intervention came in and tested you at 19 months. They suggested therapy and that's where we began. You were resistant, always swiping the toys off the high chair tray, but your therapist, Joanna, kept assuring us that there was an amazingly bright little boy in there, and we just had to find a way to "unlock" you. By 23 months, Joanna discussed increasing your hours. By Christmas you had seven hours of therapy a week. By January, that had increased to fifteen hours a week. You were having some serious compliancy issues, both with us and your therapists. You have always been a very strong-willed child, wanting everything done your way. I admire your determination, and I believe it's what helps you when things get really tough, but I also knew that it could be the barrier to your success. Increasing the hours scared me. What if it was too much, what if I wasn't letting you be a little kid and giving you enough time just to play, what if you hated me for taking all of this time away from you?

It was a tough decision for Daddy and I. We wanted to help you and we were so afraid to make the wrong choice.

There was also the issue of "to be or not to be" autistic. Everyone had an opinion, and they voiced them whether we wanted to hear it or not. We got everything from "Yes, autistic" to "He's just lazy"and "You coddle him too much." The not knowing for sure was the hardest. I prayed every night that the sick feeling I had in the pit of my stomach was just me overreacting. I told myself that if I just prayed enough, God would take all this away from us, from you, and things would be normal again, whatever that meant. In March, we took you to a developmental pediatrician so we could get a "formal" diagnosis. I can still remember sitting in during the evaluation, screaming inside, wanting you to just start talking and do all of the things the doctor asked you to do. I wanted to rescue you from her, show her how smart you were and tell her you were just having an "off" day. But I knew what the end result would be, because I had known all along. And then I heard the words....Autistic Spectrum Disorder.

She spoke for a while after that, but I couldn't make out anything she was saying. I felt like I was outside of myself, watching everything unfold. Daddy sat and listened while you played on the floor, but my body was so numb that I couldn't cry even though my heart felt like the life was being squeezed out of it. I remember getting up and leaving the office, getting on the elevator and getting to the car before I burst into tears. As strange as it sounds, I'm not exactly sure why I was crying. It wasn't as though it was some big surprise to me. Maybe it was the finality of the words, like some guilty verdict. Maybe it was just my body's way of finally letting go of the "what ifs" and "maybes". Whatever it was, I need to let you know something about your dad. Through all of this, he has been the most supportive, positive father in the world. When I started to cry, he took my hand and said, "This changes nothing." And, you know, he was so right. We were going to go home and continue doing everything we were doing, and live our lives the way we began living them months ago. The diagnosis gave us a name for what we had been working on all along. It didn't change the way we felt about you or what our goals were. And do you want to hear something so ironic? The day after your diagnosis, you said your first word, car. Unbelievable.

So here we are today. It's been a long, unpredictable journey, but five months since your diagnosis, one year since the start of Early Intervention, six dedicated therapist, and countless therapy hours later you continue to grow, change, and thrive every day. Are there days when I'm sad? Of course. The uncertainty of your future scares me because I want you to have every opportunity that life has to offer. I want you to live a full, independent life. I want you to go to a regular school and have a lot of friends. I want to watch your peewee football games every Sunday. I want to take lots of pictures as you get ready for your prom. I want the college graduation, the phone call telling me you've found "the one", the dream wedding, the kids. I want it all for you. I want to give you the world. And are there days that I'm happy? Yes And the happy days far outweigh the sad, and that is because of YOU, my son. All this therapy, all the lessons we have to teach you, and yet, you've taught me so much more in the short time you've been here. You've taught me to stop and really pay attention to the "little things" because they are actually the big things. You've taught me how to laugh,really laugh, when the world gets so crazy you want to cry. You've taught me that "perfect" is overrated. You've taught me that it's not about my plan. It's about God's plan. You've taught me to love more, complain less, and enjoy every single second on this Earth, because it's so precious. You've taught me how to be selfless, how to see the beauty in uniqueness, and how to believe again, in all things. You are my miracle, and I'd be lost without you. A lot of people talk about how great it is that Daddy and I have done so much to help "save" you, but they've got it all wrong. It's you who has saved us.

All my love always,
Mommy

The New Year's Gift

Susan Erickson

December 30 is just another Sunday. The two of us get up at our usual time and race downtown to be on time for our 10:30 AM Church Service. Danny's main reason for going to church is to "Share the Peace" just before the offering is taken. This is his time to shine. When the pastor says "let's all share the peace," Danny is out of his seat and on his way to shake hands and hug as many people as five minutes can allow. According to Danny, it is the only really good reason for going to church. And, ever since our Pastor mentioned in one of his sermons that all people are neighbors, Danny has been convinced that greeting everyone is a must for living right.

Our Sunday ritual continues after church with lunch at one of our favorite restaurants. It is among the few that Danny has chosen as his favorites. In Danny's mind we must patronize the few restaurants on his list religiously. There is no room to add another, at least not until the latest favorite's menu has been exhausted. It's OK because we've made this Danny's day; the day that makes it all worth getting up for. Let it be realized that eating is taken seriously and is not considered a leisurely activity. When Danny is done, well, that means we're both done and ready to meet our next adventure. Again, there are limited activities that we can choose from, and these are presented by Danny as the options week in and week out. Not that they can't be changed, it's just that the process takes a long time before a change is made in the agenda. And then it's very meticulously selected as an option.

On this Sunday, the choice is to go to the airport. Of course, Danny understands that since September 11, we can no longer go inside the airport to the observation deck to watch the airplanes, nor can we just simply walk around the airport, greet people, and eat lunch. He's accepted this alteration with as much calm and grace as his mind can possibly handle. I believe it's been made easier by the fact that we have a viable alternative to the airplane watching ritual, and this one has an added perk. So, off we go to the airport observation parking lot. What an incredible place this has proven to be for Danny. Now, not only can he watch airplanes take off and land, he can wave to all the cars that pass by with the one and only reward being a wave returned.

The usual ritual in the airplane parking lot goes like this. Mom (that's me) finds the parking space the furthest away from all other cars just to keep from attracting undo attention. Danny stands outside the car (regardless of the Minnesota temperature.) Incidentally, this has become a wintertime activity with other more desirable activities in the summer when we can stand on bridges and wave to cars or walk through parks and shake hands. Well, being a slight of build woman, I prefer the warmth and relaxing atmosphere of the car. This is my chance to read; listen to the radio; and, yes, sleep. Danny doesn't seem to mind, and much prefers that I stay in the confines of the car where I won't interfere with his well thought out plans. So here we are, Danny in the freezing Minnesota winter watching planes and waving to every car that passes. Me, well, I'm inside staying warm and comfortable. I've warned Danny to not wave at the cab drivers because they'll want to stop and pick him up. It happens anyway that one occasionally stops, but that's the risk he takes. He's certainly in his element here and couldn't be happier.

This particular Sunday, it's very cold. I park my car in its usual non-conspicuous spot and quickly lose myself in the fascinating book I'm reading. I know Danny is safe. After all, he's right in front of my car where I can keep a watchful eye on him. After a very few minutes of blissful reading, I look up. To my surprise there is a car parked on either side of me. My first thought is, "why do you have to park so close when you have the whole lot to choose from?" Then I begin to think that maybe we are being surrounded by airport security or FBI, "What have we done this time?" At the very moment that I'm thinking this, the woman in the black town-car on my right gets out of her car and walks over to mine. Without any warning, she opens the car door on the passenger side of my car and hands me a folded sheet of notebook paper. I'm stunned and apprehensive. She asks me to take the sheet of paper, which I hesitatingly decline, thinking that it's a complaint about Danny that I know I won't want to read. But then she says it again, "It's OK, please take it." She seems sincere enough so I take it, open it, and begin reading:

I learned a good lesson today after watching a young man with what I would say mental challenges – That is until I watched him. You see he was standing out in 16 degree weather waving at every car that passed by. As he waved he smiled and was extremely happy if someone waved back. How simple...His human contact of just a wave in return was all he needed to be happy. Such a simple act, brought such joy. – When was the last time I waved at someone? (other than him) When was the last time I simply greeted a stranger? I was sad today about a lot of things in my life – But for 10 brief minutes I was happy – every time someone waved back at this young man.

Thank You! Jinna

Feeling somewhat ashamed of my resistance to this woman, I look up as she's pulling away in her car. I wave and smile with grateful appreciation, realizing that this woman has given me the greatest New Years gift ever. She has taken the time in her day to notice the beauty and simplicity in the actions of my autistic son. She has appreciated the small gifts he so innocently brings to the people he encounters every day of his life. She has seen the teacher in him and she has observed his human worth. I know I will probably never see this woman again. Yet, she had brought into focus a life's lesson to be shared with all of us. She has reminded me of the invaluable worth that comes in the simple act of smiling at and greeting someone, whether friend, acquaintance, neighbor, or stranger. As Danny so wisely reminds me…"Everybody's a neighbor, mom, all over the world!"

Meeting Sarah Hager

Marie LaConte

When I married my Egyptian husband in 1991, I accepted two step-daughters. These two delighted me, and I would have welcomed a third, but the third child, along with their mother, died during childbirth. This is what my husband told me. Assuming the poor state of medical care in Egypt in the 80's, I reacted with sympathy, not suspicion.

Eight months later, I discovered that I had married a divorced man, not a widower, with three daughters, not two. In shock, I demanded an explanation. "Their mother is dead to my heart, and don't worry about Hager. They take care of her in Egypt."

What kind of explanation was that? I asked my step-daughters, who lived with us.

"There was something wrong with her when she was born," they told me, "but she took special medicine and now she is okay." They knew nothing more.

I had grown to love these two children, ages nine and thirteen. Their father had been a good husband, and I enjoyed the culture of Saudi Arabia, where both of us had been working when we met and married. After I got over the shock of his deceit, I started to wonder about the third girl. If she was anything like her sisters, I would welcome her. Fours years elapsed, during which I learned nothing more. Then, the birth mother decided to send Hager to live with us. My husband's mother escorted her. We didn't know they were coming until the day the plane landed.

My husband went to the airport to pick them up as I waited at home with the girls. I opened the door as I heard their footsteps on the landing. Excited and ready to welcome my new step-daughter, I couldn't help anticipating the pleasure of guiding her, loving her, helping to bring her into full feminine maturity, behind her older sisters. I knew she'd be beautiful and delightful. I was unable to have children and I knew that this girl would make our family complete.

She entered first, a four foot teddy bear, lumbering past me into the hall. As the family enjoyed their first moments together after years of separation, I stared at the slanted eyes, the slightly folded ears, and the prominent tongue. Hager had Down syndrome. My third step-daughter had Down syndrome, and I never knew. I had accepted a child sight unseen and my husband had willfully deceived me, betrayed my trust such that I would have divorced him on the spot, except for those two girls, and now the third one that desperately needed a mother.

In an instant, I saw my future before me. I knew I had stepped into a tangle of serpents that lay in wait for the day I'd try to escape. In addition to her genetic defect, 11 year-old Hager came to me emitting body odor, with dark hair dulled by dust balls, and teeth creamy yellow, an overgrowth of plaque obliterating the boundaries between her teeth.

Her face and arms were mottled from longstanding dirt. A bumpy, red rash crawled over the tops of her hands, and her skin flaked from lack of moisture. Her clothes, pulling across the back and slack in the legs, bore wrinkles from having been washed but not folded. When she spoke, her hoarse voice pronounced curse words. This was my third daughter, the one who didn't exist, the one who supposedly had died with her mother during childbirth. This was the girl I had accepted sight unseen, as another gift from God. This was the girl no one told me about.

In the months and years to follow, I would work through several difficult adjustments; first to having a Down syndrome child foisted upon me and then trying to heal my wounded marriage and nurture a child I didn't know how to nurture.

That first night, however, I cried. I cried because I didn't know what else to do. I was paralyzed with anger and disgust for my husband and pity for myself. Would I have married him if I had known about her? I felt guilt and shame because the girl was innocent, deserving of loving care just like her siblings. I cried for days, maybe weeks. Between bouts of tears, I tried to communicate with this child, whose name, Hager, displeased me more than any Arabic name I'd ever heard

For weeks, I reeled between the shock of my husband's deceit, and the embarrassment of having to reveal all this to my family. I told my husband, "If you ever, EVER, lie to me like this again, I'll leave you." I also told him, "If this child EVER disrupts my life, or causes me ANY kind of inconvenience, I will leave you."

How would I introduce Hager to my parents and relatives? "Oh, by the way, here is a third step-daughter I never knew I had. She has Down syndrome, and now she has come to live with us?" I cried for ten minutes during an expensive international phone call to my parents. They urged me to refuse this burden, leave him straightaway, and return to the States. I didn't deserve it, I didn't want it, and it should have been my decision in the first place. After all, I had not given birth to her; the moral responsibility for her existence did not fall upon my shoulders.

"But he's been a good husband," I blubbered, "and I love his other two girls."

No matter what would happen in the future, the girl needed to be bathed, properly clothed, and taken to the doctor. That first night, I showed her how to brush her teeth, and I asked her sisters to bathe her. From the shower, their echoes of playful laughter cushioned my sobs, which I did not want them to hear.

The two older girls behaved as though their sister was just like them. Would I ever be able to do the same?

The first requirement for healing was that I never forget that this girl had been victimized even more than I had. Her birth mother rejected her, and now her stepmother didn't want her. Ironically, our shared victim status caused me to feel sympathy for her. We were unlikely partners rowing the same boat, but she didn't know it. Her innocence held me together.

Later, I reached into the expatriate community for other Down syndrome mothers. I poured out my whole tearful story into their patient ears. They, not my husband, soothed me, reassured me, and gave me strength. They, not my husband, guided me to a good pediatrician and a school established specifically for Down syndrome children.

I tried to convince myself that I was just like any other mother who found out she had a Down syndrome child. Though I tried, I couldn't forget that I was not like other mothers. I had not carried this child. She was not my flesh, and she came to me not through a mistake of biology, but by the deceit of my husband. How would I overcome that blow to become an effective, loving mother to this child?

I hadn't known any Down syndrome children or mothers until Hager came into my life. Then, my days revolved around activities aimed at helping her function. Between me and myself, I had to make it right, learn to accept it. I started by educating myself. To gain some perspective, I demanded the birth records and the chromosome analysis. I learned that Hager's mom had been only twenty-six when she was born, and that the genetic defect was not an extra chromosome, as is the usual mechanism for producing the condition, but translocation, in which the extra chromosomal material attaches to the chromosome already in place. The net effect is three chromosome's worth of genes on two chromosomes. This mechanism is responsible for only 2% of Down syndrome births. So, my odd family was unique genetically as well as socially. Somehow, that knowledge consoled me.

The pediatrician, a Syrian woman, examined Hager, and told me the child was fine, free of congenital heart abnormalities common in Down syndrome children. The doctor looked at me too long, and then said, "She is lucky to have you." She might as well have run a stick through my abdomen and pinned me to wall.

I don't remember many details of those first years, and I don't remember when I started to relax and grow some affection for Hager. Though her Arabic wasn't much better than mine, communication didn't flow easily between us. She spoke the Egyptian dialect, while I was accustomed to the Saudi dialect. Her pronunciation was incomprehensible to me. We'd all been speaking English most of the time, anyway, which she had never heard before. How was this girl going to adjust to our eventual relocation to the United States?

I remembered a slogan from a twelve-step program: "One day at a time." Hager didn't mind that I didn't understand her. She wanted to be a part of every interaction. This quality would serve her well. She didn't want to amuse herself, she wanted to amuse others, and she enjoyed their attention. But one morning while she was absorbed in a television program. I decided to take advantage of the time. In the kitchen, I browsed through some cookbooks and opened the last can of Diet Pepsi. Halfway through the can, I heard her footsteps coming down the hall. I didn't want to share the last can with her, so I quickly opened the cabinet door and put the can on a shelf. But, it was too late. Her eyebrows drew down, mouth puckered in disgust, as she barked, in Arabic, "You idiot! Don't you know? Pepsi goes in the refrigerator!"

I burst out laughing. I removed the can from the cabinet and gave her the rest of it. She smiled just as quickly as she chastised me. Her emotions, always raw, always pure, and always exposed on her face, changed easily and frequently. Maybe, just maybe, I could learn to nurture this girl. I decided then that I would try. And, if things happened to work out, I would add "Sarah" to her name, and call her Sarah Hager. Sarah Hager, my third daughter.

Julie's Journey

Juanita Spencer

Julie is 27 years old, weighs 68 pounds, has brown hair and eyes and has profound mental and physical limitations. Her medical diagnosis is Rett syndrome with a seizure disorder and profound mental and motor retardation. Most test scores show her to function at 0 – 3 months of age. She has scoliosis, contractures to all limbs, receives nutrition and medications through a tube permanently placed in her stomach, does not walk, talk or care for herself in any way. While all of the above can be used to describe Julie, she is so much more than that. She is also courageous, inspiring, a teacher of patience and compassion, a giver of unconditional love, my hero and my first born child.

I could probably write nonstop for days about my journey with Julie. I've cried a million tears of sadness and anger because her life is not as I dreamed it would be, but one day I woke up and realized that those tears wouldn't solve a thing. And although I occasionally wonder what it would be like to see her fall in love and have children of her own I am able to see the beauty of her life as it actually is and I know that she is living exactly the way she is supposed to.

When I was a child our family attended church every Sunday. My first glimpse of unconditional love came from watching a woman interact with her son. This woman and her husband arrived in an old truck with their twelve children. Eleven of those children rode in the back of the truck while one special child rode in front with his parents. Rain or shine, that family came to church and eleven children marched inside and sat quietly near the back of the church. The husband strode gingerly towards the front and sat with the other preachers while his wife entered the church wearing an old brown coat and carrying a young man in her arms. The man-child's limbs were rigid and although he must have been heavy, she carried him as if he were as light as a feather. Mrs. Moore laid her son beside her on the church pew and joined the congregation in song and worship while her son cried, moaned and shook with seizures. I watched the woman pick her son up and rock him gently to try to comfort him and as I saw him become quiet and relax in her arms I could see her smile.

I couldn't have been more than ten years-old, but I can still recall the peace that I saw on her face when her son became still. To have twelve children must have carried its own burden at times, but to have one of those children be an infant forever must have been so difficult for her.

Mrs. Moore has crossed my mind many, many times as I've rocked Julie and tried to comfort her during an illness or after she shakes with seizures. Isn't it strange how something can impact our lives? Mrs. Moore will never know the strength she has given me. We never spoke directly and yet her life's story speaks to me every time I feel afraid for Julie or am so tired that I feel I can't go on.

Some people have suggested that I should place Julie in an alternative setting and get on with my life. Some people call me a martyr, but I don't think of myself as that. I simply see myself as a mother who loves her child and who simply tries to meet that child's needs. Julie and I have spent many nights in the hospital as she battles infections, pneumonia or nearly uncontrollable seizures. We've faced all her fights as a team. Each time I find myself weary to the depths of my soul, I can look at her lying in bed smiling and giggling as she watches The Little Mermaid and my spirit lightens.

We've lived in several cities in Alaska, Virginia and Texas over the past 27 years and Julie attended special education classes all along the way. In each place her disabilities have made a change in the school system. She has introduced music therapy, art therapy and even hippotherapy into school systems; thus allowing hundreds of other students the ability to benefit from her struggles. We were fortunate to work with a Physical Therapist (newly degreed) in Alaska when Julie was just a toddler. That woman became very upset with me because Julie was unable to perform some tasks during therapy sessions. She said that every child can learn to do anything and that even a dog can be taught simple things. Well, of course that PT was sent packing! Several years later that therapist came to me and begged me to forgive her. She said that Julie was her first client and that she simply didn't understand that when you are dealing with people with limitations (whether mental or physical), it is important to focus on their abilities and not their disabilities. Once more Julie's life made a lasting impact. Her life has meaning. She has worth.

I don't know what the future holds for me or Julie. I'm now 55 years-old and can feel myself slowing down. I also see Julie aging. Her body becomes more frail with every passing day. She has a few gray hairs now while I have a lot. I'll continue to care for her as long as our health permits. Thankfully, Julie is enrolled in a program that will provide an alternative homelike setting if something should happen to me. I've worried for years about where she would go if I'm no longer able to care for her. So, I now have a sense of peace about that.

Take a closer look at that car with handicapped tags rolling along down the highway. It just might be Julie and me going "bye bye". I might be singing off key to an old Tammy Wynette tune while both of us are laughing so hard we cry.

One Step at a Time

Amanda Radcliffe

Have you ever been caught in a maze? Winding around a corn field, in a themed haunted mansion, or at a house of mirrors on the boardwalk? Remember Harry Potter's adventure inside a maze in his last tale, Harry Potter and the Prisoner of Azkaban? We all know the feeling. Lost and wandering, not knowing which direction to turn, or where to go, thinking we're home free, only to find a dead end and the need to turn all the way back and begin again. So many hopeful paths explored often leading to only disappointing turn backs. Usually there's a lot of backtracking before you find your way.

That's what living with autism is like.

If I had a nickel for every time someone has asked me, "why does your son do that?" Maybe he's screaming, flapping his hands, walking up on his tippy toes or throwing a tantrum like a two year old. He is six. Maybe you've asked him a question and he just looks away. Truth be told, I don't know why he does these things. I have yet to find a doctor, therapist, teacher, or psychic for that matter who can tell me exactly what's happened with my son Callum, how he got this way, or what on God's green earth to do about it. So, when I'm asked, "why does your son do that?" I often respond that I simply don't know. That modern science hasn't figured it out yet and I'm just a worried mom trying to love him and raise him the best way I can. Finding our way, lost in a maze.

A primary challenge of having a child with autism is that no one has the answers for you. No one can tell you what the best course of treatment is for your child. How to best help them reach their potential. Each child's symptoms and needs can be so different. So we wander. We educate ourselves as best we can. Here, I must simply interject to all you kind hearted souls who call the mom of an autistic child you know when you see a snippet on TV, we're on it! You learn more than you can imagine about something that you never imagined touching your home or your family. Education encompasses so much in the world of autism; gluten & casein free diets, auditory processing, sensory integration, supplements, B12 shots, drugs galore if you are willing and a never-ending list of therapies. The list goes on and on and ends somewhere between swimming with the dolphins and Zoloft! These are the choices we are making when we should be deciding between baseball or soccer, bicycle or skateboard, Power Rangers or Batman.

So we work our way slowly through, always wishing for that bird's eye view to the finish. So many agonizing twists and turns. Some have been helpful and some have been incredible wastes of energy, money, and most importantly, time that we don't have to waste. I now fully acknowledge that a jerk can sell a desperate mother just about anything. There is no price tag on hope.

We are fortunate to have excellent professional advice. A phenomenal DAN (Defeat Autism Now) doctor, a therapeutic team leader who's as vested in our son as we are, teachers who care, a wonderfully supportive family, our sense of humor, and genuinely good-hearted friends who call when they see that snippet on TV. We are grateful.

On good days, when Cal is talking, laughing, playing with his sisters, and had a great day at school, I think for a moment that just over the hedge, I might glimpse a way out. A spot of daylight is there, visible through a small opening. Normal, or officially known as neurotypical, boys are there playing happily, waiting for Cal to join them. And then, like in Harry's infuriating maze, the way closes off and we step back again. On bad days, when Cal has hit and bit and barked and screamed, I am lost, huddled on the ground in a corner weeping and wondering what will ever become of my son. Will we ever escape the cruel labyrinth of autism?

We stood at the daunting entrance three long years ago and still we fight every day to find our way. I'm a smart and reasonable woman and I realize we may never the find the exit, but we've made progress. Hedges hurtled, obstacles crossed, demons exorcised, paths blazoned, we keep fighting forward, two steps ahead and one step back. After years of hard work, primarily his, Cal is tremendously better than he was at the age of three. We still have far to go and there is no time to rest for the weary.

I need to go, I think I spot some light just around that next corner. "Come on Callum! Let's keep going! That's it baby…one more step"

Dignity

Faith Gallatin

"God knows who the special moms are who can handle the special kids. He knew you were one of them!" A well-intentioned compliment, once again, backhands me across my soul.

There is no truth to that statement. It only shows the ignorance of the one saying it. Those of us who mother special needs kids are no different than any other mother. We dream big dreams for our kids before they are born, as well as after. We teach them everything we can. We work hard to channel their energies into appropriate outlets. We encourage mental, emotional, social, and intellectual growth. We celebrate the milestones. We grieve the temporary set backs.

Yet we are a little different from moms of typical kids. I call this nuance "dignity". Those of us who have faced the enemy of our children's challenges usually have this quality. It's one of noble bearing, conduct and character. It's a depth beyond the norm.

I'd like to use the letters of the word "dignity" to explain this journey: Denial, Investigation, Grief, Knowledge, Involvement, Therapy, and Yourself.

Denial. Been there, done that. Friday night at 7:00 pm, this pregnant lady received a call from the specialist 100 miles away stating there was something very wrong with my 34-week old baby. She didn't know what, but could I come in next Tuesday, the first available appointment, to get things checked out?

What should I pray for? That the baby is stillborn instead of living for a day or a year? That the baby will have Down Syndrome or another well-known syndrome? That the doctor was reading the wrong chart?

My husband and I didn't know what to hope for. The possibility of a special needs kid was not even on our radar. We had been married for thirteen years. We were healthy, happy, and I had been an angel during my pregnancy! I quit coffee, chocolate, and refused any medication even for a severe cold. I did everything right. The doctor must be wrong!

Sure enough, at our appointment they ruled out problem after problem. I was put on bed rest for safekeeping. I did deliver my beautiful baby girl at the metropolitan hospital in case of an emergency with her. But, once again, when she was born, they couldn't find a thing wrong! We were sure our prayers had been answered and the doctors had been misinformed. I wasn't searching for trouble where none was apparent. Life was good – albeit a little short on sleep!

Investigations rock the denial boat until you fall overboard or start rowing. My perfect toehead, blue-eyed baby girl was tested at seven months old, just for follow-up purposes. The physical therapist was very kind and gentle. But she said Heather was performing at a five-month testing level – two months behind her chronological age. I was sure this was because she was born three weeks early and was still catching up.

No, came the reply. I was advised to come back in a couple of months and start checking into resources to help move along her development. My sister-in-law, a neo-natal nurse practitioner was with me that day.

I'll never forget what she asked me. "How does it feel to be told your daughter isn't perfect?" Until that exact moment, I hadn't believed what anyone else had said; not the doctors, not the physical therapist. When Auntie Heather, who loved my daughter almost as much as I did, stated the truth I finally heard it. She had listened to her colleagues and heard what they were really saying. My daughter was developmentally delayed and needed help. Now.

I started rowing the investigation boat. Years later, I'm still rowing without a shore in sight. You see, my daughter still has no box to check on a form, no syndrome to name her delays, no official diagnosis. She qualifies for services in all areas,cognitive, speech, gross and fine motor. We deal with vision difficulties, sensory integration issues and auditory processing delays. I'm open to any theory, experimental or not, that may shed light on or potentially expand her abilities. And so the investigation continues.

Hard on the heels of investigation, which dynamites denial's excuses, comes grief. Heart wrenching, overwhelming, indescribable grief. I have been to the place where I examined everything I did that may have triggered her disabilities. I've been to the other place where I wished she had some other syndrome that was easier to deal with. I've second-guessed our choice to have another child, another girl who is typical in every way except becoming the older sister to her older sister early on in her life.

The toughest piece of grief is how it catches you at the most inopportune and unexpected moments and knocks you flat on your face. Like when I noticed she hadn't added a word to her speech in over a year. She still couldn't walk up or down stairs when her younger sister was running up them. The first day of kindergarten in her regular classroom when all the kids were talking to each other and I had to leave her without me to interpret for her. Even her sister has difficulty at times playing with her due to her lack of motor skills. I've come to realize that grief will be a continual part of my life with my daughter. It will surface as often as it can, or as often as I let it.

Knowledge takes the fear out of the unknown. Through this journey I have found asking questions, asking for clarification, and asking for information, as many times as I need to,has given me the confidence and strength to move forward.

Effective advocacy only comes through clarity and expression of thought. This position of strength only comes by understanding my daughter as thoroughly as possible and knowing I am the one person in this whole world able to get her what she needs in the way she needs it. If I don't stand in the gap for her, no one will.

Involvement is the next step. It is critical that I be there in the trenches with my daughter, going to her therapies, talking with her teachers, helping her to learn how to play with other kids and making sure that all of her providers share the same goals.

This is where the rubber meets the road. Am I willing to take action and move forward with what I have learned? Will I risk offending someone by advocating the best choice for my daughter? Do I choose the road less traveled in order to gain the opportunities I most desire for her?

The rewards are great. I see growth in her. I get to celebrate the little victories with her therapists. By being involved on a day-by-day basis, I cannot drift back to the supposed "comfort zone" of denial. I must push myself to keep her best in mind, to continue to search for the next step for her. It keeps me alert and alive.

Therapy is the support necessary to grow and reach your fullest potential. For both her and for me. I took her to therapy because she needed it physically. What I didn't know was how much I needed therapy in order to be her mom. I learned how to be a "special" mom by watching, asking, and interacting with other moms like me. As our kids played, we talked, laughed, cried, and learned from each other.

We all need the right people in our lives spurring us on to greater achievements. Those who encourage us gently – and sometimes with a swift kick in the butt. Those who keep us accountable to doing the next investigative step we are putting off because we are scared of the grief of yet another diagnosis - or lack of it. I have found a few of those friends. Our relationship is so much deeper than friendship. It is more like a "Sisterhood of Special Moms That Don't Want To Be Special Moms". Without this group of ladies, I would have given up long ago.

You. Yourself. The last letter in dignity, yet the most important. Self-care is critical to be productive in life, even more so when you have a child demanding an inordinate amount of time and energy. I am not good at self-care. Managing Heather's needs puts me into perform-ance overdrive. At first I thrived on it. I was praised for being such an involved and caring mom.

When she turned three, we still had no official diagnosis. The gaps between her skills and typically developing kids were increasing rather than decreasing. The light at the end of the tunnel was fading quickly. I would be doing this "special mom" thing for a very long time. It was no longer novel or fun.

One evening, I just snapped. I wanted to run away from everything. I couldn't hold it all together anymore. I wasn't a "special mom" and didn't want to be called one anymore. I started thinking about driving to my sister's house, almost 2,000 miles away. As I headed in her direction, something stopped me. Instead, I drove to my support group meeting. My friends saw my tear-ravaged face and gathered around me. They listened without judgment, loved me, cried with me, encouraged me to keep going. Later that night, I went home, older and wiser and, finally, committed for life to being my daughter's mom, no matter what.

Not every day is easy. In fact, some are impossible. Would I trade her? Some days, yes, but mostly no. She is my daughter. I am her mom. No one said life was fair. It's a journey where I am lucky to have my special companion to share it with.

Sweet Sixteen

Michelle S. Weil

I am planning my daughter's Sweet Sixteen Party. I don't know how many people she wants to invite. How big a deal should this be? Do you have any good ideas? I'd like it to be a bit different. I can't believe she's going to be driving. Where has the time gone?

Sixteen years ago, on a bright, crisp cold winter morning, we took that nerve-racking drive to the hospital. My labor was going to be induced. This was different than my other deliveries. We didn't know what to expect. After an excruciating long day, my third child, my baby, entered the world. Amniocenteses results months earlier declared it was time for us to have a girl. After two boys, this was very exciting. I was so excited to have this mother-daughter relationship. My husband, never having had a sister, looked forward to this new pink and ballet slipper world. We welcomed our little princess, Kimmi, with love, joy, and excitement.

The conversation about my daughter's upcoming sweet sixteen is purely a dream fantasy of mine. When December 7 creeps up, my daughter won't be nagging for the car. This is because Kimmi is mentally challenged. The general public describes this with an ugly, heart-piercing word…retarded.

In 1990, as time unfolded, I had to face that Kimmi had "issues". One counselor, who was a mother of a special needs child herself, said to me, "You will miss those "Kodak" moments and that is probably what you are so afraid of." I knew that what was destroying me was the dread of the future and what it would mean for my family and me. The pain jabbing at my heart daily was my concern. The tension gnawing at my family's happiness was my fear.

Major milestones quietly slipped by. They are tucked away in a corner of my mind. I am keenly aware of them as they try to sneak past me. They represent a promised land that I will never see. Only, once in a while when I think of a milestone, I pause to wonder how it might have been.

Sixteen is special for girls because our culture says it is so. It is emerging independence; a driver's license marks the end of carpooling and chauffeuring a child to their play dates and activities. Sixteen is a time for boyfriends.

Raging hormones are common for adolescent girls. Kimmi shares that experience. It is difficult for her and she can't make sense out of it. Explaining it to her is futile. She isn't capable of understanding this. My heart breaks for her.

Kimmi is beautiful. She has a warm, welcoming smile and a fun personality. At 5'7" tall, she is deceiving; she often appears, from a distance, as an adult. She has boundless energy. My husband and I are her best friends. We are there for Kimmi. Our goal is to maintain her happiness and to make her feel accepted in a world where she is out of place.

Celebrate her 16th birthday? Of course we will. We will go out to her favorite fast food restaurant and she will be thrilled to open her gifts. We will fuss over her and sing Happy Birthday as we enjoy our ice cream. We will go on a long relaxing ride, and play her favorite CD's. Kimmi loves that.

In the Doghouse: A Recollection

Heather Mount

He is a collector. His bedroom floor is littered with boxes containing his many treasures: marbles, hoses, rocks, bark, coins, baseball cards, half eaten candies, and rubbery swells of chewed ABC gum. The walls are covered with pictures of dogs: small dogs, big dogs and even blue dogs. The words woof and bark frame his doorways and spunky Jack Russell's cover his bed - one real, four stuffed. Wooden shelves are lined with a collection of ceramic dog banks and cookie jars. Inside the largest jar is an ample supply of dog treats for the occasional visitor. (Yes, I have found the neighbors' dogs in my house happily feasting on Snausages). His room is like a dog house; littered, cozy and crowded.

His love of dogs began four years ago when a small Jack Russell Terrier, Tizzy, came into our lives. I'll admit that Tizzy was for my older son Andrew who was feeling left out in the wake of Timmy's craziness. As an infant, Timmy cried and he cried some more, and then some more, and, for a change, he cried. If I hadn't had Andrew first, (who was an easy baby), I would have nominated myself for most incompetent mother of the year. They (the experts) said that he would out grow it. He did. The constant crying stopped and the tantrums began: monstrous, monumental, earth shattering. He would have fits about the same thing day after day, night after night. Often,he would fall asleep crying and wake up an hour later and resume. He never missed a beat. He never wanted to leave the house to do the fun baby stuff like go to the mall to gum soft pretzels or to tumble at Gymboree. My pain grew larger as each day passed.

Preschool did not go well. His teachers described him as withdrawn, uncooperative and confused. They blamed his behavior on the divorce and on my poor parenting skills. I'll call it the "look" – I received it from many people: friends, family, and strangers. The "look" said so many things: she is not consistent with him, he needs more discipline, he is so cute - what a shame, if he were my child I would... Did people really believe that I wanted my son to act this way? The dark thoughts began to settle in my mind. I replayed the pregnancy. Did I do something wrong? No it must have been the epidural – I heard they were bad. Did the grief I felt when my grandmother died sneak into my womb and hurt my son? I was so tired. I felt as if I was suspended in time, holding my breath waiting for something to happen.

When Tim was three, he climbed up onto one of the wide second story windowsills of our house. For a moment he gazed out the window and then he lied down on his back and began kicking; trying to kick his way through the glass, trying to fly away. I grabbed him and held him, unsure whose pain was greater, his or mine.

I had just adopted Tizzy one week earlier. She approached him and began to lick his face, his hands and his arms until she brushed every last bit of angry from his soul. His body grew limp in my arms. Tizzy could calm my son when he was unable to make sense of his world, when he couldn't stop his tantrum, when he left me to dwell in his angry place.

At the time I didn't understand. What did the dog know that I did not? How could slobber and stinky breath console my son when I couldn't? My touches and caresses only aggravated him, my voice like fingernails on a blackboard, my every move a failure. At that moment, I shed all of my self doubt and finally allowed myself to see my son as someone who was in pain, not as someone who was being raised improperly. Tim was different. Separate from us. Even the dog knew. I put on my armor and waged war.

Now, it was my job to convince the "experts" and everyone else that he was not going to simply grow out of this. I bought books. I read them. I made other people read them. I climbed over and conquered mountains of paperwork. I badgered and badgered until final victory. A diagnosis. I was told that Timmy had something called Sensory Integration Dysfunction. He was having difficulty interpreting all of the stimuli that he was receiving. Sounds, smells, tastes, touches all became confused once they entered his space, often overwhelming him to the point of tears, anger and deep sadness.

My feelings about this were a mixture of guilt, happiness, anger and despair. While feeling anguish, I spent a fair amount of time only "ifing". My list of only ifs was, and still is, quite extensive. I was happy that I had a name for his behavior and sad that there really was something wrong. One day I tried to imagine what it felt like to be Tim. He hated certain articles of clothing. Tormenting myself, I spent half the day in a pair of high waisted, out of style Gloria Vanderbilt jeans. (Since they were from the eighties and two pregnancies later, they were very snug.) After about twenty minutes, I wanted to lie down on the floor and cry too. I did. I looked up and found both of my sons and the dog staring at me. Wondering. "Take them off," they said, and I did. Another thought provoking moment. For the first time since his diagnosis, I saw beyond the label. I realized that there were a million things that he could do to help himself. Moral: If the jeans don't fit, don't wear them.(Believe me - Tim will not wear them.)

Tim is now seven. With help, he has learned many different ways to cope with his sensory overload. He is an incessant gum chewer – leaving deposits everywhere. One day I had to chop a huge portion of his hair off because he was stuck to his car seat. Wearing socks with sandals – allows him to kick better and have good luck. Using his upper body muscles he suspends things in midair. I will never forget the day I looked out the window to see my new kitchen stools swinging from the play set. Tree bark was strewn across my living room floor - he wanted to see if he could put the tree back together. He felt bad for it. When someone scores a goal during a soccer game, he cartwheels the length of the field. In order to figure out his world he asks thought provoking questions: Would you rather be a circus worker or a slave? Would you rather wear underwear made by elves or made by a factory? I still feel the urge to explain his behavior, but now I stop myself.

Finally, I realized that people like him just the way he is. He is not a conformist by any means, yet, he is accepted. He has taught me that what people really want is to be noticed. Even the dogs who come over to visit feel special. Can you imagine what they are thinking as they are sprawled across his bed? If they could talk, they would say: This is the life. Rub my belly some more. Do you think he will play ball with us later? Nothing better than fresh Milk Bones. Same time tomorrow? Our lives will never be normal or dull. For Tim there is no normal. Challenges are opportunities for gathering and he is a collector.

The Light at the End of our Tunnel

Candace Miller

We're at the park; my son, my daughter, and I. My daughter is play-ing quietly in the sand, filling and emptying a plastic pail. My son is shrieking in my ear. He's mad at me because I wouldn't let him dump sand on his sister. He's more than just mad. He is in a rage. Other parents, mostly mothers, are stealing glances our way. I can feel their eyes and their disapproval. How could I let him go on like that? What kind of parent am I? But don't they see my little girl? Don't they see how good *she* is? They don't. All they see is my quirky, challenging son.

A friend who has a son with special needs much more profound than my Christopher's once told me that it's probably harder to have a kid who outwardly looks like a typically developing child. She makes a good point. Neurological issues like Sensory Integration Dysfunction and ADHD can't be seen. People just see a kid who acts like a holy terror. Add in a vocabulary above age level and people think you have a horribly behaved smart kid. I often wanted to scream at the parents who looked at me askance as my son flailed about on the floor, "It's not my fault! My daughter isn't like this! I'm a good parent!"

Parents of quirky kids can spot each other a mile away. We can recognize the furtive glances that say, "Who is going to think he's weird because he won't stop spinning?" When we catch that parent's eye, we smile encouragingly. If we suspect a child has similar issues to our child's, we gently try to steer the conversation in that direction. We want and need validation. We want and need commiseration. We want and need to be understood by people who are going through the ringer like we are. It's such a relief when a parent says, "Oh, my kid seems so much like your Christopher!" They get it.

I used to feel the need to explain to every bystander that Christopher had special needs, that he was different. In the early days it was really important to me that people realized he was trying really hard to behave, he just couldn't help himself sometimes. Then it dawned on me that those people, the ones who judged me (and him), weren't worth my time. They weren't worth the explanation. I was trying to justify our lives and choices *to myself*. I even stopped telling the parents of his friends at school all about his issues. Either they liked him the way he was or they didn't.

Christopher has come such a long way in the five years we've known about his sensory issues and in the three years we've known about the ADHD. The specialists all told us he would get better, but I didn't believe them. They said he'd mature and start learning how to control himself. I'd nod and smile, but I just knew they were wrong. Things were so bad! How could they get better? But he did get better. He's doing so well nowadays that sometimes it's hard to remember those dark years when I would just sit and cry after I put the kids to bed because we'd had such a bad day. I'm so very proud of him and of us, for doing what we had to do to make our son's life better.

I still do worry about him, though. I hope that he'll be able to find his niche and I wonder if he'll have to take the medication for the rest of his life. I know that while things are good now, tomorrow or next month or next year will bring new challenges. Our struggle, **his** struggle, isn't over. I just want him to have a good life.

Thirteen Diamonds

Nancy C Anderson

My new neighbor touched my hand and said, "What a lovely ring, it looks like an antique. It's so unusual, where did you get it?"

I replied slowly, carefully choosing my words "It's custom made."

She said, "I have a friend who's a jeweler. Would you mind if I copied it?"

I smiled, "First, let me tell you the story behind the design."

It was just after New Years Day in 1990 when I found out I was pregnant with our second child. My Husband, Ron, was thrilled, but I was apprehensive. Our five-year-old, Nick, had several learning disabilities and he was quite a handful. I told Ron, "I'm afraid I won't have enough energy to take care of Nick *and* a newborn baby."

I went for all the required check ups and the doctor assured me that everything was fine. However, since I would be thirty-five when the baby was born, and that meant I had a higher chance of a baby with birth defects, the doctor wanted to do an ultrasound.

I tried to find a comfortable spot on the hard examination table as the nurse's aid squirted the cold sonogram gel on my expanding belly.

One technician slid the scope over my stomach as the other one watched the monitor. I looked at the woman who was watching my baby on the screen. Her face didn't have much expression. Then, suddenly, it did.

Her eyes widened and her hands flew involuntarily to her mouth as she made a sad squeaking sound. "What's wrong?" I asked. I sat up and repeated my question. She tried to compose herself as she scurried toward the door and whispered, "I'm sorry." The other technician left too, so I tumbled off the table and went to look at the picture that was still on the screen. I didn't see anything unusual. It just looked like a blurry negative of a skinny baby. I looked down at my stomach and rubbed it as I whispered a prayer, "Oh Lord, I think we're in trouble."

After the amniocentesis, my husband and I went back to the hospital for the test results. The doctor said, as if he were reading from a textbook, "Trisomy eighteen is a genetic disorder that always involves profound mental retardation and severe disfigurements." Then, he said the words that still live inside a tiny zipped pocket of my heart, "Your baby's condition is usually incompatible with life. Most women in your position, in order to spare themselves unnecessary anguish, just get an abortion. We can schedule yours for tomorrow morning."

I wasn't able to speak. I stopped breathing. I felt like I was drowning. I wanted to drift down into the cool dark water and disappear. A silent tear slid down my face and we left the office without a word.

My thoughts were conflicted, *I believe abortion is wrong, but I don't want to go through 'unnecessary anguish.' On my own, I don't have the strength to fall in love with a baby who is going to die.*

I kept saying it, even before I meant it. "I choose to love this baby with all my heart." I willed my words into actions as I timidly caressed my stomach. I moved my lips as I mouthed the words, "I love you." No sound came out. I kept repeating the phrase until my brain found the secret passageway to my heart and I was free to taste the bittersweet tears of loving a child who would never love me.

My mother said, "Try not to think about the future. Your baby is alive today, be alive with him. Treasure every moment."

I talked to him, sang lullabies to him, and gave him gentle massages through my skin. I knew that I might have to do my best mothering before he was born. Each day I prayed that he would live long enough to know that he is loved and that we would have time to kiss him hello...and goodbye.

Four months later, we met little Timmy face-to-face. The nurse covered his fragile, twenty-ounce body, in a soft blue blanket and matching cap. His heart monitor beeped an unsteady greeting as she handed him to me. His beautiful little rosebud mouth surprised us. It was an oasis of perfection. We held our emotions in check, knowing we had to pour a lifetime of love into a minuscule cup. Ron and I took turns rocking him as we kissed his soft cheek. Repeatedly, we told him, "We love you, Timmy." He never opened his eyes. He felt no pain. His heartbeat got slower and slower and then, reluctantly, stopped.

We kissed him goodbye.

I looked at my neighbor's tear-stained face and said, "I had this ring made within a few days of his birth. I drew a picture of what I want-

ed, told the jeweler why I wanted it and he worked late into the night to have it for me the next day." She looked closer as I explained the design. "The ring has two curved bands of gold. The longer one symbolizes my husband's arm and the smaller band represents mine. Our "arms" are holding a small, lavender alexandrite (Timmy's birthstone.)

She was silent for a long time, and finally said, "You should be the only person in the world to wear that ring. I won't copy it. Tell me about the diamonds"

"There are 13 tiny diamonds; one precious jewel for each minute that he was alive. I wear it on my "baby" finger. He's always with me."

Saving Sam

Kelley Cunningham

Sam was a difficult child from the moment he was conceived, but I was so thrilled to be pregnant after many years of treatment for endometriosis that I didn't care. It was a Friday when I went for that first ultrasound, at six weeks gestation, but it showed delayed development. The OB told me this pregnancy would not thrive. I was told to go home, wait and come back on Monday. That was a fun weekend.

I went back expecting the doctor to schedule me for a D&C but to her surprise there he was on the screen in all his beautiful, fuzzy grayness, his heart beating strongly. I was dizzy with relief and giddiness, but the pregnancy was an ordeal.

I developed diabetes even though I had no family history of the disease and was not overweight. I swelled up like a water balloon. I had preterm labor and was on Brethine to stop the early contractions. It worked TOO well; I eventually had to be induced. After a hideous two and a half hours of pushing Sam was born. He didn't breathe right away. Finally, after a minute they got him going and he was fine. But the forceps bruises on his face took weeks to fade.

Sam grew rapidly and was a beautiful baby, although a little nervous and colicky. Looking back my first clue that something was amiss should have been his Baptism day. He didn't just cry, he screamed himself hysterical. But what did I know? All babies cry at their Christenings, right? He reached all his milestones early. He smiled, pulled up, laughed, walked before the books said he should. But he didn't talk.

At his first birthday party I noticed he ignored the other kids. He didn't even seem to notice they were there. I shrugged it off and figured twelve months is too young for babies to play together anyway. But the first nagging doubt had taken hold.

Over the next few months I noticed more instances like this. And his speech wasn't really progressing. The books said boys talk later, and I wanted to believe them. I remember having a sinking feeling whenever I read how many words he should be using. Sam's vocabulary was never even close.

This is how it came on...not in one big cloudburst but rather as a storm you helplessly watch gathering on the horizon, moving closer to you by the minute. The feeling of dread is so real and palpable that it must have an atomic weight.

The sky grew even darker the day I took him to the children's zoo. All the other little kids put their hands through the fence to pet the bunnies and goats. Sam just ran up and down the fence, his head turned at a funny angle, watching the fence posts form patterns in front of his eyes.

Around this time I noticed he had learned all his letters. He would stand on his squishy alphabet puzzle floor mat and say each letter and its sound. It was eerie. No one had taught him.

But once he knew his letters I was able to teach him to read in about ten minutes. I showed him how letter sounds combine to form words. He saw it as a code and was fascinated. He read the book back to me, but had no idea what the story was about. He was like a parrot. The book was "My Many Colored Days" by Dr. Seuss. Every time I see that book now I want to puke.

But at the time we thought we had a genius on our hands, especially since his number skills were equally advanced. He could not converse with us or ask us questions, but hey, even geniuses aren't perfect!

After a month of preschool the behavior problems began. He had screaming tantrums if a routine was broken. He had strange fixations, like a compulsive drive to memorize every bridge clearance in town. He became hysterical if his favorite GMC truck was not parked in the same place everyday at the train station. He *loved* license plates. Yes, license plates.

Once at a backyard Bar-B-Q he escaped from my sight for a minute. It was dark and I was becoming increasingly panicked as I searched for him. The guests dispersed all over the dark backyard to help find him. Most ran toward the pond. I was sure he had wandered in and drowned, but no, my brother-in-law found him by the guests' parked cars. He was lovingly tracing license plate numbers with his fingers.

Searching for answers, I consulted the pediatrician. "That's why they call them the terrible twos", he told me. I just needed to be firmer with him. This was incredibly unhelpful advice as Sam was lining up toy cars precisely in neat rows as we spoke.

But the preschool was wonderful. At first they said it was a normal adjustment period. Soon the situation got worse and they had a psychologist come in. She also said Sam needed more discipline but that he was fine. Strange. I thought I was pretty strict, but perhaps I wasn't providing enough structure. I had been doing some freelance work and my hours were somewhat erratic. I had just given birth to Sam's brother Noah. Maybe all this mess was just jealousy that he could not express.

One day the preschool director handed me a stack of papers. She had printed out some information she found on the Internet, something about Hyperlexia. It's a syndrome that exists on the autistic spectrum continuum. It involves grossly impaired speech and social development, ritualistic behavior and precocious reading and number skills. As I read through the syndrome's characteristics it was as if they were describing Sam. They even mentioned a fixation with license plates. I felt sick.

As a last desperate clinging to normalcy I asked her "Don't you think this is typical two-year-old behavior?" She shook her head sadly and said nothing. I let go of my old life and fell into the abyss.

The selfish part of me entered a mourning period for the motherhood experience I would never have with Sam. I thought I would never enjoy him as other mothers enjoyed their children. Even the good days had a sense of sadness that loomed ominously. If he did something that seemed "normal" I couldn't be happy about it. I thought, *yes, fine, but he just did X and look how abnormal that was.*

I was bitterly jealous of other mothers. They seemed to glide through this motherhood thing effortlessly. It felt so heavy to me.

I flogged myself for a good long time. How did this happen? Was it the immunizations he received, the Pitocin, the forceps, the delayed breathing, the Brethine, the wine I drank before I knew I was pregnant, the Depo Lupron shots I received for Endometriosis, the morning coffee I had refused to give up, the fever I had at seven months gestation, the Diabetes, the chemical they used to clean the bronze elevator doors in my office building, the unwashed fruit I threw down one day at lunch? The fact is no one knows what causes it.

But at the same time the information I received from the school was a relief. As I read through the stack of printouts I felt strangely exhilarated. At last I knew what in the hell was going on with my little boy and what I could begin to do to help him. It became my all-consuming mission.

The preschool hooked me up with a wonderful speech pathologist. She told me that Hyperlexics learn by reading. After that I wrote everything for him. I even began to write scripts for him, like: *if someone says hello to you say hello back.* If I could find some sort of pattern or structure in an abstract issue he could begin to make sense of it.

The speech pathologist did not think Sam was autistic but clearly had "issues". I was clueless as to the process of getting him evaluated by the state for placement in the dishearteningly-named Preschool Handicapped Program in our school district. She helped me with this. The ordeal included an evaluation by an expert that diagnosed him as PDD-NOS/Hyperlexic. That's Pervasive Development Disorder, Non-Specific. A politically correct way of saying "autism, we think, but we're not really sure".

She gave me a handful of autism support group flyers and wished me luck. Afterwards I took Sam to lunch. As I watched him absently chewing his fries I felt so low I couldn't stop the tears from welling up right there in the goddamned Burger King.

So the child development expert said he was autistic, but the speech pathologist said he wasn't. His doctor said no, his preschool said yes, and everything I read pointed me in different directions.

More research online. Thank God for the bloody Internet. I read I was supposed to begin a highly aggressive program of behavior modification. I found there are trained professionals that come into your home to do this, but I couldn't afford it. I read up on it and tried to get the gist of it myself.

Maybe this was somewhat reckless but I felt I knew my kid better than any therapist. Already I had gotten different answers from different experts, so I learned to trust myself. I joined the American Hyperlexia Association. I followed the group's discussions online, gleaning tips and encouragement.

In the wonderful Pre-K Handicapped program he started to blossom. He was a smart kid who worked very hard to please his teachers. He made remarkable progress, but he still had a very long way to go.

My third son was born when Sam was four and a half years old. I don't remember much of that time at all. I was in a daze of fatigue. The strain of raising three boys born in less than five years, one with profoundly taxing special needs, was brutal on our marriage. It was all kids, all the time. Little slights blew up into battles. We found ourselves keeping track of whose turn it was to change a diaper. Luckily we were of the same mind about Sam. So many couples flounder if one parent is in denial about a child's issues, but not us. We both agreed about the course of action to take, and we trusted each other with it.

The toll this took on me was insidious. Already feeling rudderless since I left work to stay home with the kids, I began to feel overwhelmed and depressed. We couldn't afford a nanny to help out. I found myself compensating for my often joyless slog through parenting by overeating. I didn't even notice how much weight I had put on. When I did notice I didn't care. I started to drink a little too much. Never enough to be a danger to myself or my kids, but certainly more than I should have.

But it wasn't all dark. We managed to find some humor in the strangeness of our new existence. I took advantage of Sam's number fixation by convincing him he HAD to be in bed by seven-thirty. And he was, every night. I remember laughingly relating this to a mother of an NT (neurologically typical) child. She was horrified. I didn't feel badly, though. I needed child-free evenings so desperately I'm quite sure those early bedtimes saved my sanity.

Sam was able to attend a mainstream kindergarten class, but life became more complicated. He began to emerge from the fog that prevented him from seeing other kids even when they were right next to him. This was a mixed blessing; more awareness brought social confusion. He was so behind that he had no idea how to behave in a free-form game of tag that came effortlessly to all the other kids.

Each time he had a social crisis I wrote out a script for him. This is the way he eventually learned how to talk to other children. I would try to make it fun, like a multiple choice test, and make one of the choices completely silly. He would laugh at this, and at those times I felt hope. He was beginning to get it.

I spoke with his teachers at the beginning of each school year, illuminating Sam's eccentricities. They would look at me with raised eyebrows, thinking I was either nutty or way too focused on my kid. But after a few weeks we would talk again and they would be amazed at how well I knew him. I always approached it with the angle "if you do this Sam will do that and your job will be easier."

It's gone on like this for the last few years. Sam is doing amazingly well, and getting ready to enter the fifth grade. He enjoys the math enrichment class at his school, he's a top student in all subjects and he plays the piano beautifully.

All this is wonderful, but the thing that thrills me most is seeing him with his friends. The normal, bittersweet milestones of a child's life other mothers anticipate with dread are pure bliss to me. He wants to leave me and be with his friends? Yippee! He's sassing back like a normal preteen? Yahoo! He's noticing girls? Huzzah!

Sam is still "classified" as a Special Ed student even though he barely needs services anymore. Recently I sat down for a meeting at the school with his new caseworker. I found myself telling an abbreviated version of the Sam Story for the umpteenth time. I mentioned that he has come so far that perhaps he never really did have autism, or if he did he has somehow outgrown it. The caseworker smiled weakly and said "You can't outgrow it. Maybe he has just learned to compensate for it."

I felt anger simmering. I thought, *How do YOU know?* How dare she dismiss my hopeful observations so offhandedly, or profess to know the limits of my boy's abilities! Child development specialists are learning more and more about autistic spectrum disorders every year. Just thirty years ago experts blamed autism on cold, austere mothering.

I can't pretend to know what has changed in his brain or exactly how he made such progress. I can't really offer much advice. All I can do is lend a sympathetic ear. But anyone who meets him now is amazed to find out he was diagnosed as autistic. I have stopped telling them. I don't have to anymore.

But what do I tell Sam about his remarkable journey? What good will it do him to know? Knowing he has come so far should give him the confidence to tackle anything. But it just may make him feel more alienated.

For now, I'm not telling him. He hasn't asked. Maybe he never will and maybe he'll never know just what he's overcome. He'll see himself as a normal person, facing the same challenges everyone else faces. A miracle.

As for me, I'm better too. I feel like I can finally exhale. The extra weight's gone. I don't drink much anymore. I gained a profound empathy for all mothers. We may hide under cloaks of humor and stoicism but we all have our stories of glittering bravery and sheer endurance.

Sam still has many challenges ahead. Like all parents I worry about puberty but for Sam it will be harder. He still has trouble reading social cues. But his progress continues to surprise everyone. I see less and less struggle, more and more normalcy.

The other day he asked me "Mom, I don't want to hurt your feelings, because I know you used to be a girl, but I was wondering, why do they act so funny?' That's about as normal a question as you can get from an almost-ten-year-old boy.

Sam, you're going to be okay. For today, anyway.

Author Bios

Jennifer Bailey, proud mother of Ethan, has closet aspirations of being a writer. For now, she hopes to return to teaching high school English. This is her first venture into publication. Jennifer lives in Bangor with her husband, Travis LaCombe.

Kim Winters is a contributing editor for Edge of the Forest online children's literature monthly. (www.theedgeoftheforest.com). Her inspirational online journal, Kat's Eye, features musings, rants, and raves on writing, balancing work and family and life after the MFA. When she's not holding barf buckets or doing archaeological digs in her kitchen, she is working on new projects and revising her work-in-progress, a young adult fantasy novel. A graduate of Vermont College, Kim resides in Lockport, Illinois with her college sweetheart, Phil, and three children, Elizabeth, Elena and Samantha, two retrievers, Buffy and Jewel and tomcat, Mr. Ginger. For more about Kim, her writing life and current projects, visit her online journal, Kat's Eye at www.KimWinters.blogspot.com.

Chelsea Celentano lives in New Jersey with her husband, David and their two sons, Santino and Tommy. She enjoys teaching 6th grade Language Arts and Social Studies and working part-time as a scrapbooking consultant, but her real joy comes from being a full-time mom to the two sweetest boys on earth! This is her first time being published and she is both honored and humbled to be in the company of such an amazing group of women.

Marla Davishoff lives in Deerfield, Illinois with her husband, Craig and two children, Levi, 7 and Bennett, 4. She writes candidly about raising two boys with special needs, drawing upon her experiences as a mom and a social worker. Her essay "Only Human" appears in The Elephant in the Playroom. (Hudson Street Press, March 2007).

Susan Wagner is a shoe-obsessed freelance writer. She lives in Oklahoma with her husband, Wade Williams and their two sons, Henry and Charlie. You can find her on the web at www.fridayplaydate.com.

Nancy C. Anderson (www.NancyCAnderson.com) is the award-winning author of Avoiding the Greener Grass Syndrome; How to Grow Affair-Proof Hedges Around Your Marriage. She is a contributing author to dozens of anthologies including Chicken Soup for the Father and Daughter Soul, Nancy has been featured on The Montel William's Show, The 700 Club, WORLD Magazine, Our Daily Bread and Family Life Today. She lives in California with her husband of 28 years and their son, Nicholas. She can be reached at NancyCAnderson@msn.com.

Renee Bryant lives in Garden Grove, California with her five children, Brianna, 25, Elliott, 24, Ryan, 15, Katelyn, 12, Shawn, 8, and her granddaughter Alena, 4. Renee has been a guest speaker on a national Internet radio station program hosted by Dr. Judith Greenberg speaking on autism related topics, special education and the benefits of early intervention. Renee is currently writing her own story about raising an autistic child called "All Things Work Together."

Shannon Andreson is an around-the-clock-mom, full-time ASD therapist and moment-by-moment writer, editor and designer. She lives in Minneapolis, Minnesota with her supportive husband, Jason and charming son, Henry. Her writing has appeared in many local publications. She also donates her time to a Minneapolis alliance of educators and parents of children with special needs.

Susan Erickson is the mother of a 23 year-old son who has both Autism and Schizophrenia. She took an early retirement from her Minneapolis consulting firm and now spends her time freelance editing, practicing yoga (a longtime passion) traveling and writing stories that she can share with others who are going through similar experiences in raising a special needs child. Susan divides her time between her family members who live in Minneapolis and Philadelphia and also takes annual trips to Mexico and other parts of the world for leisure and exploration.

Swati Avasthi received her B.A. from The University of Chicago. After a variety of careers she has found that writing is the only one for her. In 2006 she received the Loft's Mentor Series Award. Her fiction will be published in Writer's Post Journal. This is her first non-fiction publication. She lives with her riotously funny children and incredibly supportive husband in Minneapolis, Minnesota.

Rhonda Pollero has penned more than thirty mystery, suspense and romantic suspense novels and has received numerous industry awards. She has been featured in The New York Times, The Washington Post and Cosmopolitan. She is a frequent lecturer and recognized authority on structuring the novel. In March, 2007 Rhonda's launched her hardcover debut with The Finley Anderson Tanner Mysteries with the release of Knock Off. She resides in Florida with her family.

Sheila Webster-Heard lives in Calumet City, Illinois with her husband, Douglas and three children Doug Jr, 8, Darius, 7, and Alysia, 1. Learn more at www.SheilaWebster-Heard.com.

Amanda Westphal Radcliffe lives in Pennsylvania with her three children and worked in partnership with her mother, Antoinette Westphal managing Antoinette, the Day Spa & Salon in Paoli, Pennsylvania before selling the spa to a national spa management corporation. She holds a B.A. from Moravian College.

Candace Miller-Janidlo is a wife of one and a mother of two who lives in a suburb of Cincinnati, Ohio. She is currently pursuing a degree in culinary arts and will soon return to graduate school to obtain her Master's in Psychology.

Lorena Smith was born and raised in Sri Lanka where her Swedish mother and Singhalese father run an orphanage and various social empowerment programs. She has been published in several magazines. Lorena mainly writes about life and family issues surrounding parenting special needs kids and issues women in developing countries face. Another essay can be seen in the anthology The Elephant in the Playroom. Lorena lives in Texas with her husband and two children, Alexandra, 9 and J.J., 8.

Molly Nichols graduated summa cum laude from Tulane University School of Law and practiced law for several years. She lives in North Carolina with her husband David Cortes and their four children, Patrick, John, Mary and Abby. The special challenges involved in raising John are made easier by the help of supportive friends, family and teachers and caregivers, especially Lori, Tiffany, Mary, Eileen and Kevin. Molly works as a special education facilitator and is a longtime volunteer advocate of diversity awareness and acceptance in the schools.

Heather Ristau lives in Albany, Georgia where her husband is stationed with the Marine Corps. She is the mother of three boys, Samuel, 5, Asher, 2 and new baby, Tucker. Heather has been writing stories, poems and journals since she was a child, but only recently began pursuing publication for her work. She has written a book that delves into the intensely emotional life of being a mother of a special needs child and is seeking publication. She writes daily in a blog where she is learning about codes and templates while sharing her daily MOMents. She is a maternity and infant photographer and you can find her at www.HeatherRistau.org.

Paige Huskey lives in Dayton, Ohio with her husband, three children and a beagle mutt. Paige is a recent graduate of Wright State University where she pursued her M.A. in Literature. She currently teaches, tutors and does freelance editing, but her passion is writing fiction. Paige's oldest child, now 16, has been diagnosed with Asperger's Syndrome. Paige finds great sustenance and current information from a local support group called Dayton Asperger's Resource Network (DARN). For more information on Asperger's Syndrome or DARN, please visit www.darngroup.tripod.com.

Kristen M. Scott lives in a suburb of Chicago with her husband and two teenage children, the youngest of who has Autism. Her essays have appeared in the Chicago Tribune, and other local newspapers. One of her essays was chosen for inclusion in the upcoming anthology A Cup of Comfort for Parents of Children with Autism. She leads a support group for parents to address the emotional impact of parenting special needs children and has spoken to various groups on the subject. Contact her at kscott127@comcast.net.

Juanita Spencer lives in Keller, Texas with her husband, John, daughter Julie, 27 and Kitty, the cat. Juanita's son John, 23, resides in California. It was John who encouraged Juanita to submit Julie's Journey for publication in this book saying that he felt certain the story would be accepted because it was written from the heart. As he said, "You can't go wrong with that, Mom." Juanita worked as a long distance and directory assistance operator in the Washington D.C. area for six years after high school graduation. She graduated with highest honors from the Dale Carnegie business course in 1995. She now spends her time for caring for Julie and as a bookkeeper for her husband's business. Juanita enjoys gardening and reading and has a strong belief that all human beings have a purpose in life and that we are all special in our own unique way. She firmly believes that we should grow where we are planted. Juanita can be reached at juanweta@yahoo.com.

Jenny Menn lives in Medford, Massachusetts with her husband, Eric, daughter Chloe and a dog who all relish life at warp speed. Jenny's career includes 19 years in graphic design, illustration and creative direction. Jenny and Eric traveled to Chile to adopt a beautiful 4-week old baby, Chloe, to complete the family they always wanted. Over the following year, Chloe's needs and issues increased significantly and Jenny left the corporate world to become a full-time advocate for Chloe. Today, Jenny works in a different capacity at the Wayside Youth and Family Support Network where she provides support for families within the system. While writing Eye of the Storm, Jenny realized that she had enough material to write a book someday.

Caryn Sullivan is a "parental unit" of four, who lives in Minnesota with her husband, two younger children and Cavalier King Charles Spaniel. In 1993, she put her legal career on ice after her 2 year-old son was diagnosed with autism. In the years that followed, she became the family medical crisis manager and an Internet junkie so she could hone her knowledge of autism and other assorted medical issues. Although Dancing with Despair is her first published work in 20 years, she hopes that more will follow. Publishers and other interested parties can reach her at carynsullivan@comcast.net.

Marie E. LaConte lived and worked in Riyadh, Saudi Arabia from 1986 to 1998. From this exciting period in her life springs much inspiration to write essays and creative non fiction. She writes personal journals intermittently, a practice that began in adolescence, and has turned several entries into pieces she now shares with others. She has contributed to Darkness and Light: Private Writing as Art and The Diarist's Journal. Marie now works as a medical technologist in a large Milwaukee, Wisconsin hospital, and studies Italian language for film.

Diane Eaton lives in Hazlet, New Jersey with her husband, Jonathan and their son David, 5. This is Diane's first published work. She is currently working on her own book which tells of her family's journey with Pervasive Developmental Disorder, behavioral analysis and advocating for her child within various schools and systems. Although Diane is a full-time homemaker, she is rarely home and spends her days assisting with David's daily therapies and advocating for her son.

Lisa Romeo, a New Jersey native, is a writer and mother of two. She is currently engaged in working towards a Master of Fine Arts degree in Creative Nonfiction at the University of Southern Maine. Lisa has written features, news and service articles and personal essays for consumer and trade magazines. A former public relations specialist, she holds a journalism degree from Syracuse University and worked as a freelance equestrian sports journalist for ten years. Her blog can be found at www.AskAnyMom.blogspot.com. She lives in New Jersey with her husband, Frank and two sons, Sean and Paul. She is currently at work on a memoir.

Margaret Mitchell lives in Phoenix, Arizona with six of her eight children. She teaches middle school choir. She did not write Gone with the Wind.

Michele Ackerman, M.A., B.S. lives in Mundelein, Illinois with her husband, Sam and two children Alex, 10 and Rebecca, 7. Michele is co-author of Someone Who Cares: A Guide to Hiring an In-Home Caregiver and a contributing author to two additional books on home health care. Her work has appeared in the Pioneer Press Newspapers and Caring magazine. She has over a decade of successful grant-writing experience at a non-profit organization in Chicago.

Faith Gallatin lives in Bellingham, Washington with her husband Mark and two daughters, Heather, 7, and Hailey, 5. Faith works with her husband in their real estate investing business available through www.MoneyCreekHomes.com. Faith is a board member at the Whatcom Center for Early Learning, a center serving families with children from birth to age three with developmental delays. Her daughter, Heather, is a graduate of the center and the reason Faith chose to be a part of this book.

Janice Noble lives in Loveland, Colorado and has three daughters, one son and a granddaughter. She enjoys writing and plans on publishing a children's book addressing real life issues that children with special needs face.

Jessica Thompson was born and raised in Phoenix, Arizona where she currently resides with her son Cyler, 6, who was diagnosed with an Autism Spectrum Disorder as well as Prader-Willi Syndrome. She obtained a degree in Psychology from Arizona State University in 2004 and is currently exercising her writing skills in several exploratory works. She plans to pursue a graduate degree in the near future.

Julie Adams lives in House Springs, Missouri with her husband, Chris, and her two sons, Michael, 16, and Nathan, 10. Julie is an 8th grade teacher in the Rockwood School District. She is very grateful for the opportunity to share her story and hopes it will help others parenting special needs children.

Michelle "Mimi" Weil lives in Highland Park, Illinois with her husband, Howard. Michelle works in brand management after completing her Masters in Management from Northwestern University's Kellogg School of Business. She has three children, Jerry, 24, Jonathan, 22, and Kimmi, 17, who is a resident at a facility for disabled children and adults. Kimmi spends many weekends and holidays with her family.

Erika Dahlquist lives in Golden Valley, Minnesota with her son Alex, 2. She is a full-time copywriter and although you have probably read some of her work on large company websites and in magazine ads, this is her first publication outside of a 9 to 5 job.

Andrea Harris lives in Dayton, Ohio with her two children, William, 11 and Joshua, 8. She teaches writing at Wright State University and her work has been published in the The Fogdog Review, MudRock: Stories & Tales and Dreiser Studies. She also writes a weekly column called Andrea's A Musings for a local bulletin and is currently working on a book about her experiences as a single mother. Her younger son, Joshua, was diagnosed as falling within the autism spectrum when he was three.

Other contributing authors include: Jesse Michener, Heide Kaminski, Heather Mount, Ann Curtis, Kelley Cunningham and Michele O'Neill.

Printed in the United States
91100LV00003B/28-75/A